MTA Bridge and Tunnel Officer Exam Review Guide

By Lewis Morris

D1506346

DEDICATION

This Exam Review Manual is dedicated to Isabella.

CONTENTS

ACKNOWLEDGMENTS

I would like to acknowledge the hard work and talent of Isabella who assisted with the editing and cover art for this edition.

About The Exam

The MTA Bridge and Tunnel Officer Exam is 85 questions long. The exam is multiple choice and administered on a scan-able bubble sheet. The exam tests the following sub-areas: Written Comprehension, Written Expression, Memorization, Problem Sensitivity, Deductive Reasoning, Inductive Reasoning, Information Ordering, Mathematical Reasoning, Number Facility, Spatial Orientation, and Visualization. The exam will be administered on Saturday, March 7, 2015.

Test Preparation Strategies
Beginning your Preparation

Begin preparing and studying as soon as possible. You want to engage your long term memory, which can only be done over a period of months.

Find a regular time in your schedule when you can regularly devote a half an hour or more of quiet study time, free of distractions.

Set a schedule and stick to it. Discuss your schedule with your family so that everybody understands your need for uninterrupted study time.

Start practicing your memory skills in everyday life. If you are walking and see a billboard, take 10 seconds to look at it carefully. Then, as you go about your way, try to remember details such as color, names, and dates. If you ride the subway, there are numerous opportunities to practice this method because you have so many different advertisements to view.

Study without distractions to the best of your ability. Turn off your phone. Inform people close to you that you will be unavailable during that time so that there is no expectation of a call back.

Be sure you are getting enough sleep, as this can greatly affect your concentration and memory skills. Creating a peaceful sleep environment by eliminating lights and sounds, obtaining quality pillows, and limiting nighttime activities can help. You should not eat within an hour or so before bed, and avoid caffeine and chocolate several hours before bed.

Alcohol can seriously affect your memory and concentration ability in several specific ways. Being intoxicated has been proven to negatively affect abstract thinking skills in people for at least 6 weeks! Alcohol affects sleep by contributing to sleep apnea, and many people who drink only moderately have been shown to sleep poorly. Regular use of alcohol contributes to weight gain and raises blood pressure. Limiting or stopping alcohol use entirely will assist you in many ways concerning the MTA Bridge and Tunnel Officer vetting process.

Motivate yourself. Find a way to be enthusiastic in your preparation. Prove to yourself that you can earn a high score and make the grade. Keep a positive outlook and make it a fun

Start early. Begin preparing as soon as the exam is announced.

Avoid last minute cramming. Cramming does not work, but refreshing your memory on the night before the exam does.

Give yourself enough time to complete each practice exam in a single seating, without interruptions. This will give you more confidence and provide you with a realistic expectation for the actual exam.

Develop careful reading habits. You must become an active reader. For example, rephrase each question in your own words to make sure you understand the question. Re-check your answers and make sure your choice correctly answers the question.

Don't try to memorize practice questions, instead focus on the process of reading carefully and actively.

Concentrate on the sections of the exam you find most challenging. Budget your time to practice more difficult areas.

* Take the pretest before beginning your review. This will guide you in deciding which areas to focus on.

* After reading the review material, take each practice exam. After each exam, go through your wrong answers and locate the correct answer by reading through the review material. Complete an error analysis early in your studying so that you may work through any deficiencies early enough to gain confidence in the material.

* Create a set of flash cards by taking any unfamiliar words from the glossary and putting them on flash cards. Write out the definition on the reverse side of the card.

The Night Before the Exam

Briefly study and review the practice examination questions you have already completed.
Focus on your successful responses. Your goal is to refresh your memory and reduce anxiety. Set two alarm clocks and leave an hour or so before going to bed. Refrain from looking at a computer screen for at least an hour before bed as the type of light emitted from the screen can also contribute to sleeplessness.

Getting Ready the Day of the Examination

1. Stick to your normal routine as much as possible. Some suggestions may not be in your normal routine, but they usually allow most persons to perform at their best.

2. Get adequate sleep. Most adults do best with 7-8 hours. Adopt this pattern at least several days prior to the exam. Even if you have trouble sleeping the night before the exam, don't worry. As long as you have rested well for several days leading up to the exam, your body will adjust and your performance will remain high.

3. Get up early enough to have plenty of time to have a light, balanced breakfast. Set your alarm and have a backup alarm set as well.

4. Minimize the use of outside influences (food, caffeine, nicotine, entertainment, etc.) that might over or under stimulate you. The main thing is to not do anything too radical - and not too different than what is normal for you.

5. Leave for the test early enough in order to allow for the traffic, weather, parking, etc. Work out childcare needs well in advance.

Give yourself ample time to settle in at the test site.

On the morning of the exam, log into a local traffic site, and consider using a traffic app such as "Waze" to keep updated on traffic issues. Have somebody drive you to the test, or take public transportation if at all possible. Imagine how stressful it would be if you ran into traffic and then had to struggle to find parking.

* Eat before a test. Having food in your stomach will give you energy and help you focus but avoid heavy foods which can make you groggy.

At the Exam Site

1. Listen to instructions and directions from hall monitors and test proctors. Make sure that you understand the instructions and ask questions at the designated time before the test begins if you are unsure of any aspect of what you should do during the test.

2. Use your time carefully, especially on the memorization section of the written test which is brief and closely timed. After that period you should have enough time to cover the entire test if you move through it steadily and do not spend too much time on any one question.

3. Read the questions and alternatives carefully. Do not jump to an answer before you have completely read all of the alternatives.

4. Respond to each question separately. The answer to one question is not meant to lead you to another.

5. Answer all of the questions. Use your informed judgment to make a choice between alternatives. This may feel like an "educated guess" but to the extent that it is informed, you are demonstrating a degree of knowledge and not just blindly guessing.

6. Don't worry about trick questions. None of the questions in this test is designed to be a trick question. The test is really intended to allow you to show your best on what it is assessing. Avoid reading too much into a question.

* Go to the bathroom before walking into the exam room. You don't want to waste any time worrying about your bodily needs during the test.

Immediately after the exam

As soon as you finish, find a quiet space to sit down and record your thoughts and impressions about the exam. Write down as many specific things as you can. This will help you, should you desire to take a similar exam for a different law enforcement title. This exam is very similar in format and difficulty to other exams you may later take. Recording your thoughts will assist you in developing an even better study plan for future exams.

Preparing for the Examination

Tests are given to assure selection of the most qualified persons into the MTA while providing all candidates a chance to compete fairly. The MTA will use several kinds of tests and screening methods to gauge your readiness to enter the Department. The written exam is one component of the overall selection process. Knowing the rationale for this test and having a realistic idea of the job can improve your chance to demonstrate your job potential.

This test is designed to assess:

*how well you observe things and how well you remember what you observed

* your basic writing skills

*your basic reading skills

* your basic math and logical reasoning skills..

In the days and weeks before the exam these suggestions are offered:

1. Visit the MTA Website. Make sure you understand each step in the process so you can show your very best at each stage. Get a feel for what the job is really like for a new cadet, and what it will be like to be a Law Enforcement professional.

2. Make sure that you accurately complete any forms or requirements prior to the exam.

3. Take some time every day to improve your reading and writing skills. These skills are important for effective performance as a MTA Bridge and Tunnel Officer Cadet and will be assessed by the test. Of course, these skills are also important in many other lines of work, including promotions within the MTA.

4. Practice taking other tests. This can reduce testing anxiety and improve your test taking strategies. The City of New York routinely offers School Safety, Traffic Agent, and Police Officer exams. Sign up for and take at least one of these prior to your MTA exam. This will give you valuable insight to the testing process, types of questions, and administration procedures. Many of the questions are similar to the MTA exam.

6. The more confident you are in your abilities, the better you will do on the exam. The way to become confident is to practice as many questions before the exam as possible. There is a very strong relationship between the number of practice questions completed and the score on the exam.

7. Strive to stay focused on the exam. Practice regaining focus when you feel your mind wandering. Successful test-takers are aware of when their mind wanders and have strategies for regaining focus. It is also normal for negative, self-defeating thoughts to enter your mind after a series of difficult questions. The trick here is to recognize this for what it is, and use a strategy

for eliminating the negativity. One way is to create a positive image of relaxing on the couch, watching a favorite movie after the exam. Think to yourself "I am almost there. Let's get back in the game and do this. Then I can go home and relax". Positive imagery is very powerful.

Attitude. This exam is an opportunity for you to show your skills and abilities, and a positive attitude can have an impact on increasing your test score. There are a few ways to fine-tune your attitude about taking this exam:

Look at this exam as a challenge but try not to get "stressed out" by thinking about it too much.
Remember that passing this exam is the first step in the selection process for entrance to the MTA, but it is not the only piece of information used to make that decision.

Understand the test format and requirements

1. Read all of the directions carefully.

2. Understand how to correctly use the "bubble" scan-able answer sheet. Ask for clarification if you do not understand how to take the examination.

3. Pace yourself and be aware of your timing. You are responsible for monitoring your use of the allotted time. Bring a watch and monitor it.

Understand the test question
1. Read each question carefully. Try to answer the question before you look at the choices.
If you know the answer, compare it to the available choices and pick the choice closest in meaning to your answer.

2. Recognize and make note of Qualifiers. Qualifiers are words that change a statement. Words like always, most, equal, good, and bad. In a multiple choice question, qualifiers can make an option on a test question be a correct option or an incorrect option. For example, the following two statements are nearly identical: It often rains in Los Alamos. It is always raining in Los Alamos. The first statement is true, while the word "always" in the second statement makes it false. Be aware of qualifiers that appear in a test question or in the answer options.
To tackle qualifiers you need to know the qualifier groups:
· All, most, some, none (no)
· Always, usually, sometimes, never
· Great, much, little, no
· More than, equal to, or less than
· Good, bad
· Is, is not
Whenever one qualifier from a group is used in an answer option, substitute each of the others from the group. Then you can tell which of the qualifiers fits best. If the best qualifier is the one in the answer option, then the choice is correct, if the best qualifier is another one from the family, then the answer choice is false.

2. Negatives can be words like no, not, none and never, or they can be prefixes like il-, as in illogical, un-, as in uninterested, or im- as in impatient. Notice negatives because they can reverse the meaning of a sentence. For example, in this answer option, the prefix in- in incomplete causes the statement to be false: "Because he based his research on incorrect data, his argument was imperfect."

Proceed through the questions strategically

1. Do not get stuck on words or sentences you do not understand: You may still get the main idea of the sentence or paragraph without understanding the individual word or the individual sentence.

2. Use the process of elimination: If you do not know the answer to a question, first eliminate those choices that are clearly incorrect. Then, put a mark next to each remaining choice to indicate what you think about it (e.g., maybe, likely, or probable). This will save you time, particularly if you decide to skip the question and come back to it later, by reducing the number of answers you have to reread and re-evaluate before making your final choice.

3. Guess: There is no penalty for selecting an incorrect answer in this examination, so answer every question. If the examination period is about to end and you not be able to complete all of the questions, reserve three to five minutes toward the very end of the examination period to answer these questions, even if you must guess.
While your guesses may not be all correct, the alternative is to leave these questions blank and receive no credit at all.

4. In "All of the above" and "None of the above" choices, if you are certain one of the statements is true don't choose "None of the above" or one of the statements are false don't choose "All of the above".

In a question with an "All of the above" choice, if you see that at least two correct statements, then "All of the above" is probably the answer.

How to avoid making errors

Each one of us has strengths and weaknesses concerning tests. This section will give you tools to identify and address weaknesses in your test-taking ability. The process of comparing your answers with the answer key and identifying patterns will help you tackle recurring problems with your testing skills.

The sample questions contained with each question type in this guide are very similar to the kinds of questions that will appear on the actual examination. Focus on the questions you got wrong. Read through the test taking strategies below and apply the strategies to help you avoid making the same mistakes in the future.

There are several possible reasons for choosing an incorrect answer. Seven common reasons along with suggestions to minimize repeating such errors are presented below.

Why candidates make incorrect responses

1. Bubble scanning sheet recording errors.

Since there are a limited number of questions on the examination, errors related to the proper use of the bubble sheet may lower your test score. Check yourself as you select each choice on the sheet to ensure you are marking the answer you have chosen. After you have completed the exam, if time permits review every question.

You may also miss questions because you failed to provide an answer or were forced to quickly select any answer (that is, guess) before time was called. If either of these situations happened, consider why. Possible reasons and suggestions include:

a. You may have missed a question because you skipped it and failed to return to it later. Then, by accident, you now bubble in spaces out of order. To prevent this, lightly mark your best guess and return to it later if you have time. This will serve as a bit of a placeholder to keep you on track.

b. You may have "lost track of the time" and been unaware that the examination period was about to end before you could mark any remaining unanswered questions. Check your watch frequently so that you can keep track of how much time you have left.

c. You may have been forced to make guesses for questions placed toward the end of the examination because you spent too much time working on difficult questions earlier, rather than skipping them and saving them for later. Skipping questions that are hard may give you more time with later questions that you have a better chance of answering correctly.

d. You may have skipped difficult questions but in returning to them did not save yourself time by reducing the number of answer choices (e.g., maybe, likely, or probable).

2. Misreading a question or answer by overlooking a key word or phrase. Reading too quickly can cause this. If you are a fast reader, learn how to check your reading for accuracy.

3. Not knowing the meaning of one or more key terms.
When you find a word you don't know the meaning of, reread the sentence to decode its meaning without worrying about the meaning of the unknown term. Try to understand the general meaning of the sentence or paragraph. The meaning of the word should become clear once you understand the general meaning of the sentence around it. Study the glossary, as it will give you a solid working background of law enforcement terms.

4. Having difficulty telling the difference between the important and unimportant parts of a question because it is complicated or difficult to understand.
First, these are the questions you should skip until the end of the test.
Second, break up the question into smaller parts; then concentrate on one part at a time. When you return to these difficult questions, first read the possible answers before reading the questions. This helps you to direct your concentration while reading the question.

Also, focus on the topic sentences that are usually the first and last sentences in a question. Read these difficult questions twice.

The first time, read for the general idea. Do not waste time on challenging words or phrases you do not understand. The second time, read for more detailed understanding. The first reading will give you the general meaning so that the second reading will be easier. Finally, try to visualize what the question is asking by drawing a mental picture of what is going on in the question.

5. Not knowing how to combine different types of information. This is a problem of re-arranging information in the correct way so that it makes sense. Use your finger to underline important pieces of information in the question on the screen and then compare this information with the possible answers point-by-point. Concentrate on eliminating the wrong answers first.

6. Choosing an answer simply because it "looks" good. Several factors may cause you to choose incorrect answers that "look good":

a. An incorrect answer may contain exact wording from the original question.

b. An incorrect answer may contain a phrase or sentence from the original question, but presented in in a different way. For example, a fact that is negated in the question may be presented as positive in an answer choice.

c. An incorrect answer may overstate what the question has stated. For example, if the question states, "Some perpetrators...," the incorrect answer may state, "All perpetrators ...."

Some strategies for avoiding the tendency to select incorrect answers that "look good" include:

a. Come up with your own answer before you review the answer choices. This will make you less likely to choose an answer that just "looks good."

b. Rate the likelihood of each probable answer before choosing one. Think in terms of "That's it!", "Probable", "Not Likely", "No Way!".

c. Beware of choosing answers based on common sense or previous knowledge and experience. Answer only on the basis of the material presented in the test question itself. In this sense, your experience can work against you.

d. Stick strictly to the facts or rules described in the test question itself. Carefully watch out for words such as "only," "never," "always," "whenever," "all," etc. and if you see one of these terms, take a few seconds to check that you understand the implications of the word in the question.

e. Beware of answers containing exact words or phrases from the question material. Do not assume that such answers are correct.

f. Prepare a defense for your answer choice. Find something in the test question that will allow you to give a strong defense for your particular answer choice. How would you explain your answer to another person?

7. You may not know why you missed a question. If you just do not know why you missed a question, we suggest you review the preparation guide again. Also, talk with someone else who may be taking the test to compare answers and information or ask a tutor, friend, or a family member for help.

* Read the question before you look at the answer.

* Come up with the answer in your head before looking at the possible answers, this way the choices given on the test won't throw you off or trick you.

* Eliminate answers you know aren't right.

* Read all the choices before choosing your answer.

* There is no guessing penalty, so always take an educated guess and select an answer.

* Don't keep on changing your answer. Usually your first choice is the right one, unless you misread the question and have become certain of the answer.

How to beat Testing Anxiety

What is Testing Anxiety?
Test anxiety is an intense kind of nervousness that arises from the total test situation. Our bodies produce chemical and physical changes in response to important events in our lives. In a sense, testing anxiety is our body's way of telling us that something really important is about to happen. As a result of this heightened state of readiness and awareness, we feel the pressure of the upcoming exam in many ways that can cause us unease and discomfort. At times, these feelings may become overwhelming and negatively affect the test-taker's performance on the exam.

What Causes Testing Anxiety?
The pressure to get a good grade, the high-stakes nature of an exam, the perceived difficulty of the exam, and the cost of the exam all contribute to the feelings of test anxiety.

What are the Physical Symptoms of testing anxiety?
- sweating palms and forehead
- sore neck and back from tense muscles
- headache
- nausea
- increased heart rate
- difficulty sleeping

What are the Mental Symptoms of testing anxiety?
- anger
- being "short" with family, friends, and coworkers
- mental blocking (drawing a "blank" on questions)
- having difficulty focusing on exam questions during the test
- feeling sleepy and yawning during the exam
- doing poorly on an exam, even though you were confident in the material
- having difficulty remembering the definitions of key terms during the exam
- mind is wandering during the exam
- negative thoughts invade your thinking

How can I reduce testing anxiety?

- Practice, Practice, Practice. With enough practice answering similar questions, you will become desensitized to some of the anxiety producing stimulus.
- Learn the material over a long period of time vs. attempting to "cram" for the exam. By studying material over a month or more, you will engage your long-term memory. This type of memory is less affected by testing anxiety.
- Duplicate the testing environment as closely as possible and practice in that environment.
- Visit the testing site if possible.
- Take similar exams prior to taking your exam. (For example, take an upcoming Police Officer exam a month or two before the MTA B & T Officer exam. This will boost your confidence, and desensitize you to anxiety producing stimulus. It will also familiarize you with testing policies and increase your stamina).
- learn to focus on the material by focusing on important terms and concepts from the glossary and practice questions.
- create a detailed study plan and schedule
- organize your study materials to eliminate frustration looking for them
- learn and use relaxation techniques such as stretching, breathing, posture, and walking

How can controlling the study environment help manage testing environment?

- Set up your study environment so that it is conductive to learning and reduces stress. Find an area that has no interruptions and noise.
- Set up lighting so that there are no shadows or excessive brightness that cause squinting or straining of eye muscles. If possible, add an incandescent cool white bulb to the lighting to help balance the colors.
- Control the temperature so you are comfortable but alert.
- Choose a chair that is not too comfortable to cause drowsiness and has a straight back to enhance postural breathing.

- Do not study in bed. Your brain is conditioned to sleep in bed and your sessions will not be as productive. Your sleep may also be disturbed by studying prior to sleep.
- Have everything necessary to work close at hand.

How can I prepare for testing anxiety?
- Recognize it as a serious part of test preparation
- Develop a study plan and stick to it
- Study long term over a period of a month or more
- Stay positive
- Take things day by day, one step at a time
- learn an effective strategy for actively chasing away negative thoughts. Learn how to recognize them and have a specific visual image to confront them with.
- don't worry. Worrying is a waste of time and energy. As soon as you begin to feel worried, grab a book and do a few easy practice questions to move forward and boost confidence.

How do I confront testing anxiety when it occurs during the test?
- Stay engaged in the exam. Force your mind to focus.
- Slow down. Anxiety changes our perception of time and tends to cause us to rush.
- Breathe. Practice sitting straight with good posture and breathe deeply and slowly. If necessary, purse your lips while exhaling to reduce your breathing rate.
- Feeling tense can be helpful. Recognize that it is your body gearing up to do its best.
- Stay in control.
- Remember. The exam will pass quickly enough. Your job is to slow things down and stay in the game as long as possible.

How can I use reinforcing self-statements to manage testing anxiety in the future?
After the exam, write down your feelings. Focus on the positive elements of the experience. This will most likely not be the last test you take in your life, and creating a positive image in your mind will help you minimize test anxiety in the future. Focus on positive

self-statements such as "I Did It!", "It wasn't that bad", "Studying really helped.", "Some of the questions were challenging, but almost fun.", and "The test was like a puzzle to solve".

How can goal-setting help me manage or eliminate testing anxiety?
- Keep your goals realistic for studying. It is easy to be too optimistic about how much time you can devote to studying. When you can't study as much as you planned, it is then easy to become discouraged.
- Be sure your goals are your own. Don't allow friends and family to pressure you into something you don't really want to do.
- Try not to juggle too many goals at one time. If you want to prepare for an important exam, try putting off other major commitments until the exam has past.
- Write your goals down. Be specific here. Describe in detail what you want to accomplish and what you are willing to do to earn this achievement. Try to keep a journal. In the journal, log your experiences and time studying. Record your thoughts and "A-ha! moments" as you learn along the way.
- Your goals should all have a definite expiration date.
- Your goals should be as specific and measurable as possible. There should be an exact, concrete outcome in mind. For example, a goal might be: "I will earn a score of at least 98% on the MTA B & T Officer candidate exam no later than on March 7, 2015. This goal has a specific, measurable outcome with a clear expiration date.

How can effective time-management help us eliminate testing anxiety?
- Begin by charting and calculating where your time goes every day. Chart what you do for a week. Look for dead spaces in time. Do you watch TV for a few hours a day? How much time do you spend on Facebook? Perhaps you like to watch a lot of sports and commentary. Also find out how much time you spend sleeping and getting ready. Investigate if there are people in your life who suck up your time. Once you have identified areas of your day that are

not used efficiently, look for ways to limit the time lost and begin using it to study. After careful study, you will be amazed at how much free time you actually have to use studying.

- Buy a day planner and chart out all of your responsibilities. Carry this with you everywhere. Complete it in pencil, and do not feel bad if you have to adjust it. Even if you find yourself wasting time here or there, record it. The purpose here is not to deny yourself free time or relaxation, it is to look for areas of time you currently waste, and fill it with more productive time spent studying.
- Keep an eye out for procrastination. It is easy to get lazy or be afraid, and procrastination creeps in. The way to manage this is to start with an easy, short question set. Do a few questions and then go back to whatever it was that you were doing before. You will find, that after a while, it will become easy to get going once you know how to start.
- Learn how to say "NO" to friends, family, and coworkers. "Time-takers" are everywhere. Look out for them and keep them at bay. Learn how to return calls when no one will answer so you can leave a voicemail that says "sorry I didn't call you sooner, I was studying......". Tell people what you are up to and promise to be around after the test.
- Put your phone on silent for the time you are studying.
- Schedule ahead. Find out what important events are coming up and plan to study around them.
- Work backwards from the test date in your planning. First, black out any important dates such as holidays or family events. Then plan for short study and practice sessions. If possible, plan back a month or more.
- Also plan specific time to practice relaxation and fitness. Schedule regular stretching, yoga, or walking. Plan your meals carefully. This is not the time to start a drastic weight-loss program. It is the time to plan regular, nutritious meals that will support your learning and memory. Foods high in energy and healthy fats should be included. Foods high in processed sugar should be avoided.
- By planning your time wisely, you may find that studying actually buys you more "free" time and less wasted time.

How do we manage the effects of perfectionism or obsessing over the exam?

Some test-takers have the tendency to obsess over an exam. This obsession could be a strong motivator to study, but oftentimes it becomes paralyzing. If this speaks to you, you are going to have to learn how to moderate your feelings. By scheduling thoughtful blocks for studying and then learning how to clear your mind, you will have a better chance of overcoming this. When setting a goal, define what result you are aiming for, and what you are willing to put in to achieve the goal. Once set, stick to the plan and learn how to be satisfied with your effort.

How do we overcome procrastination?

- Most people procrastinate. Very few people can self-start consistently day in and day out.
- For some people, however, procrastination is paralyzing and persistent. There are several reasons for procrastination.
- Time management. Many people just can't seem to balance their schedule to allot consistent time for studying. By the time they do sit down to study they are exhausted or they are so wrapped up in their affairs to concentrate.
- Negative beliefs or emotions. Perhaps you performed poorly on another exam recently. The bad feelings and fear of failure drive you to delay working.
- Feeling overwhelmed. The exam seems too big and complex.
- Personal problems. Marriage, health, job situation, finances. All of these issues creep in and take the learner off task.
- Difficulty concentrating. This issue can have many causes including diet, sleep, and outside stress. Learning how to control the physical environment is key to overcoming this issue.
- Boredom. Let's face it, studying is rarely thrilling. The way to overcome this is to start with short sessions and increase the study time as you go along.
- Fear of failure. Many people allow themselves to quit before they even start.

Why doesn't cramming work well?
Cramming is defined as studying intensely just prior to an exam. It generally includes an unfocused, disorganized last-ditch attempt to learn material typically covered over a long period of time. Cramming often results in sleep deprivation, exhausted eyes, and an overwhelmed short-term memory. Often times, a test-taker will study the entire night before and arrive at the test site weary and unable to focus. Beyond the physical discomfort of cramming, there are very good reasons for spreading out studying from a brain function and memory point of view. Successful test-takers know that the long term memory is engaged during an exam. The only way to develop long-term memory of subject matter is to study over a long period of time.

What is the difference between short-term and long-term memory?
Short-term memory is also called "working memory". It is used when actually doing something or performing a skill. Testing engages Long-term memory and is best developed over a period of weeks or months.

When we cram, what information is remembered, and what is forgotten?
Cramming has been well studied. It is very clear that while cramming, the first and last items are remembered, while the material studied during the middle of the session is forgotten. The speed at which a person reads is also significant. The slower the reading, the more material is remembered. Also, if the reader pauses regularly to mentally restate what was read, the retention of information will be better.

What is the serial position effect?
The serial position effect is the tendency of a person to recall the first and last items in a series best, and the middle items worst. This effect is most apparent during cramming. When charted, the amount of retained material forms a U-shaped curve with the beginning and end retained the most.

What is the primacy effect?
This is the tendency for the first items presented in a series to be remembered better or more easily, or for them to be more influential than those presented later in the series. If you hear a long list of words, it is more likely that you will remember the words you heard first (at the beginning of the list) than words that occurred in the middle.

Why does reading slowly while cramming help?
Reading slowly while cramming can help you retain more information because there is a tendency to repeat and rehearse the material. This will help you process the material to a deeper level and retain more.

What are some tips for cramming?
- Study the most important information first and last. Study the least important information in the middle.
- Draw up a clear plan and break your studying up into segments.
- Focus on Key terms and Vocabulary
- Read slowly. This will help you re-read and rehearse the information.

What about rumors?
Looking online at forums about the exam can be informative and helpful. Be careful, however, not to buy into the negativity that also exists on the forums. I recommend not visiting them for a few weeks leading up to the exam. It is too easy to get "psyched out" and start second-guessing yourself.

Can I "Beat" a test?
Simply put, No. The exam is professionally made and extensively field tested. The only way to beat the test is to practice numerous similar questions and, if possible, take similar exams such as the Traffic Agent, Court Officer, or School Safety Agent exams. Practice and experience are key.

How do I overcome negative thoughts?
When under stress, it is completely natural to experience negative thoughts. The key to overcoming these thoughts is to first recognize them when they occur, and second, have a specific visualization to think of when the negative thoughts creep in. For example, if you hit a hard string of questions, you might begin thinking that you are going to fail. Try to imagine yourself back at home in a few hours, eating your favorite take-out food, watching your favorite movie.
Visualization is an effective method for reducing anxiety, especially when combined with physical relaxation techniques such as deep breathing, stretching, or yoga. The more specific and focused your imagery is, the more effective it will be.

What about yoga, deep breathing, posture, and walking?
Relaxation strategies can be very effective at relieving testing anxiety. Learning how to breathe properly and keep good posture during the exam will increase your energy levels. If you are studying and begin to feel stressed, learn several slow stretches that help your posture and keep your back muscles supple. Yoga can be very beneficial, but you don't have to go out and join a studio. Start simple and incorporate balance into your routine.

Testing Anxiety Assessment Tool

Read through the responses below and assign a 0,1, or 2 indicating how much this statement reflects your feelings, 0 being none and 2 being great. Keep in mind that questions 1-10 are physical indicators and questions 11-20 are behavioral indicators.

1. I get a knot in my stomach before an exam	
2. I feel nauseous before an exam	
3. I get sweaty palms before an exam.	
4. I feel shaky before an exam.	
5. I have trouble sleeping the night before a test.	
6. My heart rate is increased before a test.	
7. I get pains in my neck and back prior to an exam.	
8. I lose my appetite before a test.	
9. I get headaches before a test.	
10. I feel fatigued before a test.	
11. I answer questions too fast	
12. I make careless mistakes	
13. I can't focus during the exam, my mind wanders.	
14. During the exam, I can't recall information I thought I knew.	
15. I worry about how everybody else is doing on the exam.	
16. I have difficulty understanding the test directions.	
17. I worry about past failures while taking test.	
18. I feel like I am running out of time on tests, even though I still finish with time left over.	
19. I feel like I studied the wrong material before the test.	
20. After a test, I suddenly remember the correct answers to questions I struggled with.	

If you score between a 0-10, you do not have test anxiety. If you score an 11-20, you have mild test anxiety, which can be a healthy motivator and can easily be managed. If you score 21-40, you need to be aware of how this can affect your performance and life leading up to the exam. By using the strategies presented in this guide and seeking assistance, you can overcome even the most severe anxiety. Take a few minutes to carefully think about and write down the causes of your anxiety. Then review the guide to find possible strategies to overcoming your anxiety.

In what ways do I suffer from the most anxiety?
A. _____
B. _____
C. _____
D. _____

What are some strategies to help me overcome this anxiety?
A. _____
B. _____
C. _____
D. _____

Examination Sub-Areas

Written Comprehension: Understanding and interpreting sentences and paragraphs.

Written Expression: Writing words and sentences in a manner that can be understood by other people.

Memorization: Remembering facts, names, numbers, images and procedures.

Problem Sensitivity: Identifying when something is wrong or is about to go wrong. It includes being able to identify parts of the problem or the entire problem.

Deductive Reasoning: The process of reasoning from one or more general statements to reach a logically certain conclusion.

Inductive Reasoning: A logical process in which several pieces of information, are combined to obtain a specific conclusion.

Information Ordering: Following set of rules or actions in a certain order. The set of rules is given. The things to be put in order can include numbers, letters, words, pictures, and procedures.

Mathematical Reasoning: adding, subtracting, multiplying and dividing quickly and correctly.

Number Facility: Solving mathematical word problems.

Spatial Orientation: Determining where you are in relation to an object or where the object is in relation to you.

Visualization: Imagining how something would look when it is moved or when its parts are rearranged.

Written Comprehension

This section tests your ability to understand written language. It involves understanding of individual words as well as sentences and paragraphs. It tests the ability to read a description of an event and understand what happened and understand the meaning of a passage. These passages are typically incident reports, policies, procedures, descriptions of events, and accident reports. These passages will be approximately 100-200 words in length and will be followed by several test questions.

Strategies for Answering Written Comprehension Questions
A. One of the most useful techniques involves reading the test questions and possible answers before reading the passage. This will help you identify and focus on the information that is being sought. You may find that you locate the answer to one of the questions related to a passage before you even finish reading the passage for the first time. If so, answer the question right away. As you go from one sentence or paragraph to the next, you may have to look back at the questions to remind yourself of the details for which you are searching.

B. Another technique is to circle key words in the passage after you have read the questions related to the passage. For example, if the questions related to the passage ask for information about a particular person (e.g., Mrs. Smith), then circle Mrs. Smith's name when you come to it in the passage so you don't waste time looking back through the passage later.

C. A third technique is to read for understanding and without becoming bogged down by individual words that you do not understand. Sometimes the meaning of a word can be decoded from the context in which it is used, or you may not need to understand the word to understand the passage. Try substituting difficult words with simpler words to help you make it through a tough passage.

D. Try to form a picture in your mind as you read. Visualization can be an important tool because it will help you "see" what is being written about and help you identify blanks in your understanding.

E. Ask yourself questions as you read. When you finish reading a paragraph or a long sentence, ask yourself what the passage was saying. What was the main idea of the reading? What was the author trying to say?

F. Use Context Clues when encountering difficult or unfamiliar words. Look at the surrounding words for clues to its meaning. Most of the time, the rest of the paragraph will give you a good idea as to the meaning of the particular word.
Often times, while taking a law enforcement exam, you will encounter words that or new or strange to you. When you encounter a word you don't know as you are reading, you can use the surrounding words to help you determine what the word means. Using the words around it is using context clues. Even if you can't figure out the exact definition, phrases and words should be able to help you make an educated guess about the word's meaning.

As you go through the question set that follows, you may know many of the words. If that is the case, try to answer the questions without looking at the answer choices. Then go back and check your answers. If you get stuck on the meaning of a word, you can look it up in the glossary in the back of this review guide.

1. Even though Roger was not directly involved in the crime, he was proven to be an _____ because he helped to provide the getaway car.

A. Accessory   B. Felon   C. conspirator   D. Burglar

2. The suspect made an _____ supporting the charges after hearing the victim speak of the pain he inflicted.

A. dialogue   B. monologue
C. admission   D. denial

3. The perpetrator's violence and intimidation of the victim led to the charge of _____ Assault.

A. minor   B. aggravated   C. simple   D. outrageous

4. Once young man was placed in custody, he was formally placed under _____.

A. lockdown   B. containment   C. arrest   D. stasis

5. A special team of police officers is used to locate fugitives and serve them with an _____.

A. arrest warrant   B. takedown
C. subpoena   D. notice of charges

6. The man was charged with _____ after intentionally setting his business on fire to claim the insurance proceeds.

A. arson   B. assault
C. vandalism   D. aggravated assault

7. The man was charged with _____ after attempting to stab another man in the back with a 10" cleaver.

A. assault   B. battery   C. arson   D. robbery

8. The kids were charged with _____ after grabbing at an elderly woman's purse and then fleeing when she fought them back and held onto her purse.
A. robbery   B. attempted robbery   C. assault   D. battery

9. The officers called for _____ when they realized that the accident deeded more officers to secure the perimeter and protect the public.
A. SWAT   B. canine   C. back up   D. ESU

10. The nurse's aide was charged with _____ after she was shown on a camera hitting and the elderly woman who was confused.
A. assault   B. battery   C. robbery   D. menacing

11. When the officer ran her license, he found that the local court had a _____ out for her because she failed to appear at her last DWI hearing.
A. bench warrant   B. statement of arrest
C. subpoena   D. deed

12. The breathalyzer showed that she had a _____ of .1%, twice the legal limit.
A. BAC   B. DWAI
C. BWI   D. DUI

13. The officer used a _____ to help determine the driver's blood alcohol content.
A. breath assure   B. blood analyzer
C. breathalyzer   D. bag valve mask

14. The man who entered and intended to steal a television was charged with
A. robbery   B. assault   C. fraud   D. burglary

15. The victim of the _____ said a man ran up and forced her out of her car.
A. robbery   B. battery   C. carjacking   D. menacing

16. _____ Protective Services was called to investigate the suspected neglect of the young person.
A. Elderly   B. Domestic   C. School   D. Child

17. The driver received a _____ for reckless driving which required they appear in court.
A. citation   B. warrant
C. writ of Habeas Corpus   D. misdemeanor

18. A _____ was brought against the delivery driver who caused the damage to the owner's hedges to make him pay for the damage.
A. criminal case   B. civil action
C. felony   D. misdemeanor

19. The gang used _____ by threatening to hurt the boy in order to get him to beat up his classmate.
A. battery   B. assault   C. coercion   D. aggravated assault

20. The council of clergy were included in the _____ who held a vigil protest the rise in violent crime in the community.
A. community stakeholders   B. rabble rousers
C. troublemakers   D. volunteers

21. In the case of an assault, the _____ is generally the victim.
A. felon   B. criminal   C. complainant   D. perpetrator

22. The storekeeper came in and signed a _____ after his store was vandalized.

A. affidavit   B. complaint   C. warrant   D. bench order

23. The young man made a _____ after he saw photos of the crime scene he created.

A. affidavit   B. complaint   C. warrant   D. confession

24. The crime family committed a criminal _____ when they made an agreement with the neighboring family to sell drugs on the border of their territory.

A. felon   B. conspiracy   C. complainant   D. contempt

25. The man was held in _____ of court for violating the judges' order of protection by stalking his former girlfriend.

A. felon   B. conspiracy   C. complainant   D. contempt

26. The man was caught with several bottles of illegal drugs and was charged under the _____ act.

A. felony   B. misdemeanor
C. controlled substance   D. conspiracy

27. Once the perpetrator was apprehended, he was brought before the _____ in order to face the charges against him.

A. court   B. public defender
C. civil judge   D. clerk

28. The homeless man had no money, therefore he was given a _____ to defend him against the charges.

A. district attorney   B. court appointed attorney
C. corporation counsel   D. detective

29. The district attorney brought a _____ against the perpetrator to seek justice for the victims.
A. civil action   B. affidavit
C. warrant   D. criminal action

30. The victim of the hit and run expired before making it to the hospital and was classified as _____.
A. DOB   B. DOA   C. DBA   D. ABA

31. The youth gang were classified as _____ for their criminal acts and refusal to go to school.
A. delinquents   B. fugitives   C. felons   D. seditious

32. The _____ was assigned to investigate the homicide after the crime scene was processed.
A. ESU   B. SWAT   C. detective   D. Sargent

33. The owner and host of a loud and raucous party was charged with _____ for disturbing the peace.
A. civil action   B. disorderly conduct
C. breach of trust   D. conspiracy

34. The drug dealer was charged with _____ after being videotaped selling cocaine.
A. conspiracy   B. distribution of a controlled substance
C. sedition   D. assault

35. A driver can be charged with _____ if their blood alcohol content is above the legal limit.
A. DWI   B. BWI   C. Assault   D. Battery

36. The suspect's confession was obtained under _____ after he was held for 48 hours and denied food, water, and sleep.
A. the influence   B. warrant   C. supervision   D. duress

37. The officer's primary role at a crime scene after ensuring the safety of the public is to collect _____.
A. insurance paperwork   B. evidence
C. registration   D. ownership documents

38. An _____ order was issued to return the fugitive back to his home state.
A. release   B. parole   C. extradition   D. deportation

39. The murderer was charged with a _____ for his egregious act.
A. felony   B. misdemeanor C. violation D. civil case

40. The DWI conducted a random _____ on drivers leaving the football game.
A. alertness tests   B. field sobriety tests
C. blood test   D. searches

41. Stop and _____ is a program in which officers stop and search people for weapons and drugs.
A. check   B. frisk   C. hold   D. arrest

42. The man's killer was charged with _____.
A. assault   B. battery   C. homicide   D. coercion

43. The case of the chop owner shooting and killing an armed bandit was ruled _____ because the owner's life was threatened and he used a registered weapon to defend himself.
A. homicide B. manslaughter
C. battery   D. justifiable homicide

44. The grand jury handed down an _____ because it found enough evidence to formally charge the woman with the crime.

A. verdict   B. indictment

C. warrant   D. writ of Habeas Corpus

45. The gang used _____ to threaten the store owner not to testify as a witness in an assault case.

A. intimidation   B. collusion C. influence D. collaboration

46. The officer went outside of his _____ when he pursued the bank robber into the next state.

A. juris prudis   B. neighborhood

C. jurisdiction   D. comfort zone

47. A young person is considered a _____ when they are under the age of 18.

A. felon   B. fugitive   C. adult   D. juvenile

48. All arrested people are first brought to the _____ where they are fingerprinted and photographed.

A. precinct   B. court C. cafeteria D. lockup

49. The bank robberies all had the same _____. The robber was alone, carried a silver automatic handgun, and spoke in a western accent during all of the robberies.

A. DWI   B. DOA   C. M.O.   D. MRE

50. The boat driver was charged with _____ after accidentally killing a swimmer while operating his vessel at a high rate of speed, in a reckless manner.

A. BWI   B. homicide   C. manslaughter D. assault

51. The child was considered a _____ by the court and therefore could not be held responsible for her actions.
A. adult   B. minor   C. felon   D. victim

52. A crime that is less serious than a felony is considered a
_____.
A. assault   B. battery   C. misdemeanor   D. probation

53. The youth was let off easy by the judge because it was his first
_____.
A. offence   B. felony   C. affidavit   D. warrant

54. The offense of double parking is considered to be a
A. felony   B. misdemeanor
C. violation of parole   D. petty offense

55. The accused consented to the use of a _____ in order to prove he was telling the truth.
A. EKG   B. ECG   C. breathalyzer   D. polygraph

56. The officers stated that they had _____ to search the man because they stated he had a pistol shaped bulge in the waistband of his pants.
A. warrant   B. reasonable cause
C. probable cause   D. officer's prerogative

57. The _____ acts as the attorney for the state in a criminal case.
A. prosecutor   B. defendant
C. plaintiff   D. public defender

58. The highway patrol officer used _____ to determine the speed of the oncoming vehicle.
A. Echo ranging   B. RADAR   C. SONAR   D. RADIO

59. The perpetrator was charged with _____ after the victim said he forced himself on and had unwanted sex with her.
A. assault   B. battery   C. manslaughter D. rape

60. The man was considered a _____ because he was charged with six DWI's in 3 years.
A. felon   B. recidivist   C. menace   D. parolee

61. The officers all assembled for _____ prior to their morning tour where they heard the daily announcements.
A. roll call   B. morning coffee   C. assembly D. lineup

62. The judge signed the _____ so that the detectives could search the drug dealer's apartment.
A. bench warrant   B. search warrant
C. parole order   D. extradition order

63. The girls were charged with _____ after they were caught stealing cosmetics from the convenience store.
A. assault   B. battery   C. grand larceny D. shoplifting

64. The crime could not be prosecuted because the _____ had expired ten years ago.
A. statue of jurisdiction   B. statute of revenue
C. jurisdiction   D. statute of limitations

65. The burglar was charged with _____ after he was caught in possession of a necklace reported stolen from the house.
A. theft   B. assault   C. battery   D. neglect

66. The driver was issued a _____ after he was observed crossing the double solid yellow lines.
A. bench warrant   B. search warrant
C. subpoena   D. traffic ticket

67. The _____ of the bullet brought it from the street level, through the apartment window where it struck the man's arm.
A. velocity   B. arc
C. speed   D. trajectory

68. The burglar was charged with _____ after he was found inside the apartment by its lawful owner.
A. unlawful entry   B. assault
C. battery   D. menacing

69. The stenographer was able to repeat the testimony of the victim _____.
A. paraphrase   B. verbatim   C. veritas   D. pro bono

70. The judge issued an _____ calling for the arrest of Barney Jones for the crime of assault.
A. subpoena   B. search warrant
C. arrest warrant D. writ of habeas corpus

71. The woman was an excellent _____ because she could recall very accurate details of the perpetrator, the victims, and the crime scene.
A. felon   B. parolee
C. witness   D. administrator

Answer Key:

1. A, 2. C, 3. B, 4. C, 5. A, 6. A, 7. A, 8. B, 9. C, 10. B, 11. A, 12. A, 13. C, 14. D, 15. C, 16. D, 17. A, 18. B, 19. C, 20. A, 21. C, 22. B, 23. D, 24. B, 25. D, 26. C, 27. A, 28. B, 29. D, 30. B, 31. A, 32. C, 33. B, 34. B, 35. A, 36. D, 37. B, 38. C, 39. A, 40. B, 41. B, 42. C, 43. D, 44. B, 45. A, 46. C, 47. D, 48. D, 49. C, 50. C, 51. B, 52. C, 53. A, 54. D, 55. D, 56. C, 57. A, 58. B, 59. D, 60. B, 61. A, 62. B, 63. D, 64. D, 65. A, 66. D, 67. D, 68. A, 69. B, 70. C, 71. C

Sample Reading Comprehension Question

"Many of our nation's highways have evolved from older routes that were originally simple paths used by Native Americans prior to the arrival of the Europeans. Today, these roads are overused and under maintained. Most roads were never properly designed and instead have only been patched or updated when absolutely necessary. The road infrastructure today is crumbling, and the toll in deaths and injury is staggering. Today, our roads are overcrowded and dangerous."

Which one of the following statements concerning the yearly toll of traffic accidents is best supported by the passage above?
A. Higher speed is the root cause of most accidents.
B. DWI should be considered a "misdemeanor".
C. It does not shock us as much as it should because the accidents do not all occur together.
D. It has resulted mainly from the condition of the roads.

SOLUTION: To answer this question, evaluate all the choices.

Choice A: Nowhere in the passage does it say that speed is a cause of accidents.

Choice B: Nowhere in the passage is DWI mentioned

Choice C: The passage does not speak specifically to "shocking" us nor does it mention the timing of the accidents.

Choice D: This passage is about the poor condition of the roads and their relationship to accidents. "D" is the correct answer.

Reading Comprehension Question Set
Directions: After reading the selection below, choose the alternative which best answers the question following the selection.

Read the passage below and answer the questions that follow:
In newer vehicles with air brakes, you put on the parking brakes using a diamond-shaped, yellow push-pull control knob. You pull the knob out to put the parking brakes (spring brakes) on, and push it in to release them. On older vehicles, the parking brakes may be controlled by a lever. Use the parking brakes whenever you park. Never push the brake pedal down when the parking brakes are on. If you do, the brakes could be damaged by the combined forces of the springs and the air pressure. Many brake systems are designed so this will not happen. But not all systems are set up this way, and those that are may not always protect the brakes from overpressure damage.
In some vehicles a control handle on the dash board may be used to apply the brakes gradually. This is called a modulating valve. It is spring-loaded so you have a feel for braking action. The more you move the control lever, the harder the spring brakes come on. They work this way so that you can control the brakes if the service brakes fail. When parking a vehicle with a modulating control valve, move the lever as far as it will go and hold it in place with the locking device.
When main air pressure is lost, the parking brakes come on. Some vehicles, such as maintenance trucks, have a separate air tank which can be used to release the spring brakes. This is so you can move the vehicle in an emergency. One of the valves is a push-pull type and is used to put on the spring brakes for parking. The other valve is spring loaded in the out position. When you push the control in, air from the separate air tank releases the spring brakes so you can move. When you release the button, the spring brakes come on again. There is only enough air in the separate tank to do

this a few times. Therefore, plan carefully when moving. Otherwise, you may be stopped in a dangerous situation when the separate air supply runs out.

1. In newer vehicles, the parking brake is controlled by
A. A blue knob
B. A yellow, diamond shaped knob
C. A red, hexagon-shaped knob
D. A lever on the dash

2. The parking brakes are
A. Hydraulic
B. Cable
C. Spring
D. Air

3. In older vehicles, the parking brakes may be controlled by
A. A lever
B. A yellow knob
C. an air tank
D. A blue knob

4. Use parking brakes
A. when parking on a hill
B. when parking to check the apparatus
C. when parking at a transfer station
D. All of the above

5. Why shouldn't a driver apply the brake pedal while the parking brakes are on?
A. The brakes may release
B. The vehicle may get stuck
C. The pressure may damage the brakes
D. The vehicle may "jump"

6. A modulating valve is used to
A. apply the brakes gradually
B. "dump" the brakes
C. lock the brakes
D. engage the antilock brakes

7. A modulating valve is
A. spring-loaded to give the user a "feel" for the braking action
B. computer controlled
C. automatic
D. a component of ABS

8. When parking a vehicle with a modulating valve
A. leave the valve off
B. move the lever all the way and lock it in place
C. pump the valve before applying the brake
D. move the lever to the middle and lock it in place

9. When main air pressure is lost
A. the emergency brakes kick in
B. the modulating valve activates
C. the brakes come on
D. the brakes become inoperable

10. The purpose of the separate air tank is to
A. allow the vehicle to be moved to safety if main pressure is lost
B. allow the vehicle to operate as usual
C. boost the air pressure
D. enhance the ABS system when carrying a heavy load

Answer Key:
1. B, 2. C, 3. A, 4. D, 5. C, 6. A, 7. A, 8. B, 9. C, 10. A

Read the passage below and answer the questions that follow:
Truck tractors built on or after March 1, 1997, and other air brake vehicles (buses, trailers, and converter dollies) built on or after March 1, 1998, are required to be equipped with antilock brakes. Many commercial vehicles built before these dates have been voluntarily equipped with antilock brakes. Check the certification label for the date of manufacture to determine if your vehicle is equipped with ABS. ABS is a computerized system that keeps your brakes from locking up during hard brake applications. Vehicles with ABS have yellow malfunction lamps to tell you if something isn't working.

Tractors, trucks, and buses will have yellow ABS malfunction lamps on the instrument panel.

Trailers will have ABS malfunction lamps on the left side, whether on the front or rear corner. Dollies manufactured on or after March 1, 1998 are required to have indicators on the left side.

On newer vehicles, the malfunction lamp comes on at start-up for a bulb check, and then goes out quickly. On older systems, the lamp could stay on until you are driving over five MPH.

If the lamp stays on after bulb check, or goes on once you are underway, you may have lost ABS control at one or more of the wheels.

In the case of towed units manufactured before it was required by the Department of Transportation, it may be difficult to tell if the unit is equipped with ABS. Look under the vehicle for the electronic control unit (ECU) and wheel speed sensor wires coming from the back of the brakes.

ABS is an addition to your normal brakes. It does not increase or decrease your normal braking capability. ABS only activates when wheels are about to lock up.

ABS does not necessarily shorten your stopping distance, but it does help you keep the vehicle under control during hard braking.

1. Truck tractors built on or after _____ must have air brakes.
A. March 1, 1996
B. March 19, 1997
C. March 1, 1998
D. March 1, 1978

2. Trailers built on or after _____ must have air brakes.
A. March 1, 1996
B. March 19, 1997
C. March 1, 1998
D. March 1, 1997

3. How do you determine if your vehicle has ABS brakes?
A. Check the registration
B. Check the certification label
C. Ask your supervisor
D. Check the inspection sticker

4. The purpose of ABS is to
A. keep the vehicle stopped when parking
B. help the vehicle climb hills without rolling back
C. help the vehicle stop without locking up the brakes
D. increase the stopping distance.

5. How does a vehicle with ABS indicate a problem to the driver?
A. A yellow warning lamp
B. A beeping sound
C. A red flashing light
D. The brakes lock

6. Where is an ABS malfunction lamp located in a Tractor?
A. On the right of the dashboard
B. On the instrument panel
C. Near the emergency brake pull
D. On the outside right of the vehicle

7. Trailers with ABS have a malfunction indicator on the
A. Right rear
B. Right front
C. Front center near the brake lines
D. Left side

8. On newer vehicles, the malfunction lamp goes on at startup and then
A. Stays lit to indicate proper function
B. goes off after driving 5 mph
C. goes off after driving 5 miles
D. goes off quickly

9. If an ABS malfunction lamp goes on while underway it means
A. ABS may not function at one or more wheels
B. the brakes are no longer working
C. brake pressure is lost
D. you must stop immediately

10. ABS activates
A. every time you brake
B. only when you are braking on a hill
C. every time you brake in the rain
D. whenever you are about to lock up the wheels while braking

11. ABS will
A. always shorten stopping distance
B. help keep the vehicle from losing control while braking
C. always lengthen stopping distance
D. increase stopping power

Answer Key:
1. D, 2. C, 3. B, 4. C, 5. A, 6. B, 7. D, 8. D, 9. A, 10. D, 11. B

Read the passage below and answer the questions that follow:
To be a safe driver, you need space all around your vehicle. When things go wrong, space gives you time to think and take action. To have space available when something goes wrong, you need to manage space. While this is true for all drivers, it is very important for large vehicles. They take up more space and they require more space for stopping and turning.

Of all the space around the vehicle, it is the area in front of the vehicle- the space you're driving into, that is most important.

You need space ahead in case you must suddenly stop. According to accident reports, the vehicle that trucks run into most often is the one in front of them. The most frequent cause is following too closely. Remember, if the vehicle ahead of you is smaller than yours, it can probably stop faster than you can. You may crash if you follow too closely.

In order to avoid hitting a vehicle in front of you, you need at least at least one second for each 10 feet of vehicle length at speeds below 40 MPH. At greater speeds, you must add 1 second for safety. For example, if you are driving a 40 foot vehicle, you should have 4 seconds between you and the vehicle ahead. In a 60 foot vehicle, you should you need 6 seconds. Over 40 MPH, a 40 foot vehicle needs 5 seconds and a 60 foot vehicle needs 7 seconds.

To know how much space you have, wait until the vehicle passes a shadow on the road, a pavement marking, or some other clear landmark. Then count off the seconds like this: "on thousand and one, one thousand and two" and so on, until you reach the same spot. Compare your count with the rule of one second for every ten feet of length.

If you are driving a 40 foot truck and you count only 2 seconds, you are driving too close. Drop back a little and count again. After a little practice, you will know how far back you should be. Remember to add 1 second for speeds over 40 MPH.

1. Large vehicles require
A. more space in front
B. more space behind
C. more space on the sides
D. more space all around

2. The space around your vehicle that is most important is
A. the space in front
B. the space behind
C. the space on the sides
D. all sides are equally important

3. You need space ahead
A. to see safely at night
B. to stop suddenly if necessary
C. to use fuel economically
D. to keep a steady speed

4. According to accident reports, the vehicle trucks run into the most is
A. the one behind while backing up
B. the one in the right hand blind spot
C. the one in the left hand blind spot
D. the one in front of it

5. According to accident reports the most common cause of trucks running into a vehicle in front of them is
A. excessive speed
B. tired driver
C. DWI
D. following too closely

6. If a vehicle in front of a truck is smaller than the truck, it can most likely

A. stop faster than the truck

B. stop slower than the truck

C. stop at the same rate as the truck

7. While driving a truck at 30 MPH, in a truck that is 50 feet long, how many seconds apart should the truck be from the vehicle in front of it?

A. 3 seconds

B. 4 seconds

C. 5 seconds

D. 6 seconds

8. While driving a truck at 50 MPH, in a truck that is 50 feet long, how many seconds apart should the truck be from the vehicle in front of it?

A. 3 seconds

B. 4 seconds

C. 5 seconds

D. 6 seconds

9. While driving a truck at 30 MPH, in a truck that is 60 feet long, how many seconds apart should the truck be from the vehicle in front of it?

A. 3 seconds

B. 4 seconds

C. 5 seconds

D. 6 seconds

10. While driving a truck at 50 MPH, in a truck that is 60 feet long, how many seconds apart should the truck be from the vehicle in front of it?

A. 3 seconds

B. 4 seconds

C. 5 seconds

D. 7 seconds

11. When driving a truck, how many seconds do you add to your following distance time when travelling at speeds above 40 MPH?

A. none

B. 1 second

C. 2 seconds

D. 3 seconds

12. When driving a truck, how many seconds do you add to your following distance time when travelling at speeds below 40 MPH?

A. none

B. 1 second

C. 2 seconds

D. 3 seconds

Answer Key:

1. D, 2. A, 3. B, 4. D, 5. D, 6. A, 7. C, 8. D, 9. D, 10. D, 11. B, 12. A

Read the passage below and answer the questions that follow:
Driving too fast is a major cause of fatal crashes. You must adjust your speed depending on driving conditions. These include traction, curves, visibility, traffic, and hills.

Perception Distance + Reaction Distance + Braking Distance = Total stopping Distance

Perception distance is the distance your vehicle travels in ideal conditions, from the time your eyes see a hazard until your brain recognizes it. Keep in mind certain mental and physical conditions can affect your perception distance. It can be affected greatly depending on visibility and the hazard itself. The average perception time for an alert driver is 1.75 seconds. At 55 MPH this accounts for 142 feet traveled.

Reaction distance is the distance traveled in ideal conditions before you physically hit the brakes in response to a hazard seen ahead. The average driver has a reaction time of 1 second. At 55 MPH this accounts for 61 feet traveled.

Braking distance is the distance your vehicle will travel, in ideal conditions, while you are braking. At 55 MPH on dry pavement, with good brakes, this can be 216 feet.

Total stopping distance is the minimum distance your vehicle will travel, in ideal conditions, with everything considered including perception distance, reaction distance, and braking distance, until you can bring your vehicle to a complete stop. At 55 MPH, your vehicle will travel a minimum of 419 feet.

Slippery surfaces will increase the stopping distance and total stopping distance significantly.

1. The distance a vehicle travels from the time your eyes see the hazard until your brain recognizes it is the
A. Perception distance
B. Reaction distance
C. Braking distance
D. Total stopping distance

2. The distance a vehicle travels from the time your brain recognizes a hazard until your foot hits the brakes is the
A. Perception distance
B. Reaction distance
C. Braking distance
D. Total stopping distance

3. The distance a vehicle travels while you are braking until it completely stops is the
A. Perception distance
B. Reaction distance
C. Braking distance
D. Total stopping distance

4. The distance required from the time moment your eyes see a hazard until your vehicle completely stops is the
A. Perception distance
B. Reaction distance
C. Braking distance
D. Total stopping distance

5. In ideal conditions, the total stopping distance for a vehicle traveling at 55 MPH is
A. 61 feet
B. 216 feet
C. 419 feet
D. 142 feet

6. In ideal conditions travelling at 55 MPH, the perception distance for an alert driver is
A. 61 feet
B. 216 feet
C. 419 feet
D. 142 feet

7. In ideal conditions travelling at 55 MPH, the reaction distance for an average driver is
A. 61 feet
B. 216 feet
C. 419 feet
D. 142 feet

8. In ideal conditions travelling at 55 MPH, the braking distance for dry pavement with good brakes is
A. 61 feet
B. 216 feet
C. 419 feet
D. 142 feet

9. In ideal conditions travelling at 55 MPH, the total stopping distance for an alert driver on dry pavement with good brakes is
A. 61 feet
B. 216 feet
C. 419 feet
D. 142 feet

10. Slippery surfaces will
A. increase total stopping distance
B. increase perception distance
C. decrease reaction distance
D. decrease total stopping distance

11. The average driver has a reaction time of
A. .75 seconds
B. 1 second
C. 1.75 seconds
D. 2.75 seconds

12. An alert driver has a perception time of

A. .75 seconds

B. 1 second

C. 1.75 seconds

D. 2.75 seconds

Answer Key:

1. A, 2. B, 3. C, 4. D, 5. C, 6. D, 7. A, 8. B, 9. C, 10. A, 11. B, 12. C

Read the passage below and answer the questions that follow:
Causes of fires can be Accidents, under-inflated or damaged tires, fuel leaks, or cargo. Preventing fires on your truck includes a pre-trip inspection, en route inspection, following safe procedures, and caution while fueling.

Knowing how to fight fires is important. Drivers who don't know what to do have made fires worse. Know how the fire extinguisher works. Study the instructions printed on the extinguisher before you need it. Here are procedures to follow in the event of a fire. Follow them in order:

1. Pull off the road. The first step is to get the vehicle off the road and stop. In doing so:
Park in an open area, away from buildings, trees, brush, other vehicles, or anything that might catch fire.
Do not pull into a service station.
Notify emergency services of your location and condition.

2. Keep the fire from spreading. Before trying to put out the fire, make sure it doesn't spread any further.
With an engine fire, turn off the engine as soon as you can. Don't open the hood if you can avoid it. Shoot foam through the grill, or from the engine's underside.
For a fire in the cargo box, keep the box closed. Do not open the unit, as it will add oxygen to the fire.

3. Select the correct type of fire extinguisher.
Type A fires are wood, paper, and ordinary combustibles. Use water or dry chemical extinguishers.
Type B fires are Gasoline, Oil, Grease, or other flammable liquids. Use carbon dioxide or dry chemical extinguishers. Do not use water as it might spread the fire.
Type C fires are electrical fires. Extinguish with carbon dioxide or dry chemicals. Do not use water, as the risk of electrocution is

present.

Type D fires are fires in combustible metals. Certain metals such as magnesium and sodium can burn. Use specialized dry chemicals including type K extinguishers to put out this type of fire.

4. Extinguish the fire.

When using an extinguisher, stay as far away from the fire as possible.

Aim at the source or base of the fire.

Position yourself upwind. Let the wind carry the extinguisher to the fire.

Continue until whatever is burning has been cooled. Absence of smoke or flame does not mean the fire cannot restart.

1. The steps in dealing with a fire in order are:

A. Select the correct type of extinguisher, Extinguish the fire, Keep the fire from spreading, Pull off the road.

B. Pull off the road, Keep the fire from spreading, Select the correct type of extinguisher, Extinguish the fire.

C. Pull off the road, Keep the fire from spreading, Select the correct type of extinguisher, Extinguish the fire.

D. Keep the fire from spreading, Select the correct type of extinguisher, Pull off the road, Extinguish the fire.

2. Preventing a fire on your truck includes

A. overinflating tires

B. spilling fuel

C. pre-trip inspection

D. disregarding safety procedures

3. To keep a cargo fire from spreading,

A. provide oxygen to the fire

B. open the hood

C. open the cargo box to air it out

D. limit the amount of oxygen getting to the fire

4. A garbage fire of burning wood and paper can be extinguished using a type _____ extinguisher.

A. A

B. B

C. C

D. K

5. A piece of magnesium machinery is on fire. Use a type _____ extinguisher.

A. A

B. B

C. C

D. K

6. There is an electrical fire. Use a type _____ extinguisher.

A. A

B. B

C. C

D. K

7. There is a fuel leak which has caused a fire. After turning off the fuel flow, use a type _____ extinguisher.

A. A

B. B

C. C

D. K

8. Why shouldn't you use water on an electrical fire?
A. It might spread it
B. You might get electrocuted
C. It might damage the equipment
D. It might spread the fire.

9. Why shouldn't you use water on a gasoline fire?
A. It might spread it
B. You might get electrocuted
C. It might damage the equipment
D. It might spread the fire.

10. How should you aim a fire extinguisher at a fire?
A. At the top of the flames
B. From downwind
C. At the base of the fire
D. In a circular fashion above the flames

Answer Key:
1. B, 2. C, 3. D, 4. A, 5. D, 6. C, 7. B, 8. B, 9. A, 10. C

Read the passage below and answer the questions that follow:
Drinking alcohol and then driving is very dangerous and a serious problem. People who drink alcohol are involved in traffic accidents resulting in over 20,000 deaths every year. Alcohol impairs muscle coordination, reaction time, depth perception, and night vision. It also affects parts of the brain that control judgment and inhibition. For some people, one drink is all it takes to show signs of impairment.

It is the alcohol in drinks that affects human performance. It makes no difference whether that alcohol comes from "a couple of beers," or from two glasses of wine, or two shots of liquor. All of the following drinks contain the same amount of alcohol:

- A 12 ounce glass of 5% beer
- A 5 ounce- glass of 12% wine
- A 1 ½ ounce shot of 80-proof liquor

Alcohol goes directly into the blood stream and is carried to the brain. After passing through the brain, a small percentage is removed in the urine, perspiration, and by breathing, while the rest is carried to the liver. The liver can only process one-third an ounce of alcohol per hour, which is considerably less than the alcohol in a standard drink. This is a fixed rate, so only time, not black coffee or a cold shower will sober you up. If you have drinks faster than your body can metabolize them, you will have more alcohol in your body, and your driving will be more affected. The Blood Alcohol Concentration (BAC) commonly measures the alcohol in your body.

1. How many people are killed every year in alcohol related traffic accidents?
A. 10,000   B. 20,000   C. 30,000   D. 40,000

2. According to the passage, alcohol impairs
A. muscle strength
B. cardiac volume
C. reaction time
D. breath rate

3. According to the passage, it takes how many drinks for some people to show signs of impairment?
A. 1   B. 2   C. 3   D. 4

4. How many 5-ounce glasses of 12% wine is two 12-ounce glasses of 5% beer equal to?
A. 1   B. 2   C. 3   D. 4

5. According to the passage, what body organ is responsible for processing alcohol?
A. Brain   B. Liver   C. Stomach   D. Blood stream

6. How much alcohol can the liver process in one hour?
A. 1 drink   B. 1/3 ounce   C. 2 ounces   D. 1 ounce

7. According to the passage, the only thing that will sober a person up is
A. time   B. black coffee   C. exercise   D. a cold shower

8. "BAC" stands for
A. Blood Area Concentration
B. Blood Alcohol Combination
C. Blood Area Combination
D. Blood Alcohol Concentration

9. 6 ounces of 80 proof liquor is the equivalent of _____ drinks.
A. 2   B. 4   C. 6   D. 8

10. A 10 ounce glass of 12% wine is the equivalent of _____ 1 ½ ounce shots of 80 proof whisky.
A. 1   B. 2   C. 3   D. 4

Answer Key:
1. B, 2. C, 3. A, 4. B, 5. B, 6. B, 7. A, 8. D, 9. B, 10. B

Read the passage below and answer the questions that follow:
All drivers should know something about hazardous materials.
You must be able to recognize hazardous cargo, and you must
know whether you can haul it without having a hazardous
materials endorsement on your CDL license.
Hazardous materials are products that pose a risk to health, safety,
and property during transportation.
You must follow many rules about transporting hazardous
materials. The intent of the rules is to
- Contain the product
- Communicate the risk
- Ensure safe drivers and equipment

Hazardous Materials are differentiated by their classification.

1	Explosives	Ammunition, Fireworks, Explosives
2	Gases	Propane, Oxygen, Helium
3	Flammable	Gasoline, Acetone
4	Flammable Solids	Matches, Fuses
5	Oxidizers	Ammonium Nitrate, Hydrogen Peroxide
6	Poisons	Pesticides, Arsenic
7	Radioactive	Uranium, Plutonium
8	Corrosives	Hydrochloric Acid, Battery Acid
9	Misc. Hazardous Materials	Asbestos, Formaldehyde

Placards are used to warn others of hazardous materials. Placards
are signs put on the outside of a vehicle that identify the hazard
class of the cargo. A placarded vehicle must have at least four
identical placards. They are to be put on the front, rear, and both
sides. Placards must be readable from all four directions. The must
be at least 10 3/4" square, turned upright on a point, in a diamond
shape. Cargo tanks and other bulk packaging display the

identification number of their contents on placards or orange panels.

1. The passage defines a hazardous material as
A. any dangerous product
B. an infectious material
C. products that pose a risk to health, safety, and property during transportation
D. any product that might explode or cause injury upon contact with the driver

2. One stated intent of the rules is to
A. contain the product
B. advertise the risk
C. ensure alert drivers
D. prevent tired drivers

3. An example of a class 1 material is
A. asbestos
B. gasoline
C. ammunition
D. uranium

4. An example of a class 3 material is
A. asbestos
B. gasoline
C. ammunition
D. uranium

5. An example of a class 6 material is
A. asbestos
B. arsenic
C. ammunition
D. uranium

6. An example of a class 7 material is

A. asbestos

B. gasoline

C. ammunition

D. uranium

7. Asbestos is in the same class of material as

A. uranium

B. gasoline

C. formaldehyde

D. hydrogen peroxide

8. Ammonium Nitrate is in the same class of material as

A. uranium

B. gasoline

C. Ammunition

D. Hydrogen Peroxide

9. Plutonium is in the same class of material as

A. uranium

B. gasoline

C. Ammunition

D. Hydrogen Peroxide

10. Pesticides are considered to be

A. Poisons

B. Radioactive

C. Gases

D. Flammable

11. Oxygen is considered to be
A. Poison
B. Radioactive
C. Gas
D. Flammable

12. Uranium is considered to be
A. Poison
B. Radioactive
C. Gas
D. Flammable

13. Gasoline is considered to be
A. Poison
B. Radioactive
C. Gas
D. Flammable

14. According to the passage, placards are used to
A. alert authorities to inspect a cargo
B. warn others of hazardous materials
C. warn drivers to stay back
D. calculate driver's rate of pay

15. A vehicle must have _____ identical placards.
A. 1 B. 2 C. 3 D. 4

16. A placard must be
A. 8 ½" x 11"
B. 9" x 9"
C. 10 ¾" square
D. A red triangle

Answer Key:
1. C, 2. A, 3. C, 4. B, 5. D, 6. B, 7. C, 8. D, 9. A, 10. A, 11. C, 12. B, 13. D, 14. B, 15. D, 16. C

Written Expression

This question type involves using written language to communicate information or ideas to other people. These other people might include any individuals with whom the MTA B & T Officer might come in contact with such as judges, supervisors, accident victims, and criminals. This question type tests vocabulary, distinctions between words, grammar and the way words are ordered in sentences. Examples might include explaining the reason for a traffic summons to a motorist, the process of an arrest to a perpetrator, or the description of an accident to a commanding officer.

For these questions, it is important that the answer correctly conveys the content of the original idea, and also expresses the idea in a clear manner. While reading the question, ask yourself: "What is the best way to say this".
The best way to prepare for this type of question is to practice writing short paragraphs that explain an idea or procedure.

Tips to help you improve your verbal expression skills:
Think of your task during this part of the exam as of being a proofreader or editor. Read slowly and thoughtfully. One strategy is to read the paragraph backwards. This is particularly helpful for checking spelling. Start with the last word on the paragraph and work your way back to the beginning, reading each word separately. Because the content or grammar won't make any sense, your focus will be on the spelling of each word.
Separate the text into individual sentences. This will help you to read every sentence carefully. Read each sentence separately, looking for grammar, punctuation, or content errors.
Notice each punctuation marks. As you examine each one, ask yourself "is this punctuation correct?"
Read slowly, and read every word. Try mouthing the words without making any noise. This forces you to think about each word and how the words work together. When you read too fast, you will skip over errors.
Make a point of reading every day. As you read, frequently stop and try to mentally put the information you are reading into your

own words. Try to verbally restate what you have read. As you read, practice locating the subjects and verbs of various sentences. Try to determine why a certain verb is required to complement a particular kind of subject.

As you read, make a list of unfamiliar words. Afterwards, look up these words in the dictionary and write down their definitions in a notebook. By writing down these words and their definitions, you will be able to remember them more easily.

Study and learn the words in the glossary found in the back of the book. Many of the terms are found on the exam and are appropriate for many law enforcement exams. Having a strong familiarity with these terms will increase your confidence level.

Grammar Punctuation, and Spelling

Below are some basic spelling rules that should help you prepare for the exam.

1. Using I Before E

Use *i* before *e*, except after *c*, or when sounded as "a" as in "freight" and "weight."

EXAMPLES: chief, fierce, and thief; deceive, receive, friend, and collie.

COMMON EXCEPTIONS: sufficient, species, efficient, weird, height, neither, science, caffeine

2. Dropping the Final E

Drop the final *e* before a suffix beginning with a vowel (*a, e, i, o, u*) but not before a suffix beginning with a consonant.
EXAMPLES:

make + ing = making

time + ing = timing

like + able = hoping

peace + ful = peaceful

base + ment = basement

encourage + ment = encouragement

COMMON EXCEPTIONS: ninth, judgment, and wisdom

3. Changing a Final Y to I

When a word ends in **-y**, usually change the **-y** to **-i** when you are adding a suffix if the **-y** is preceded by a consonant, but do not change it if the **-y** is preceded by a vowel or if you are adding the suffix **-ing**

EXAMPLES:

study + ed = studied

panty + es = panties

destroy + ed = destroyed

try + ed = tried

try + ing = trying

enjoy + ing = enjoying

community + ies = communities

COMMON EXCEPTIONS: daily, memorize

4. Doubling a Final Consonant

Double a final single consonant before a suffix beginning with a vowel when *both* of these conditions exist:

(a) a single vowel precedes the consonant;

(b) the consonant ends an accented syllable or a one-syllable word.

EXAMPLES:

mop + ing = mopping

nag + ed = nagged

grin + ing = grinning

beg + ed = begged

submit+ tal = submittal

remorse + ful = remorseful

5. S never follows X. Example "box".

6. The vowel Y, not I is used at the end of a word. Example "by".

Most Common Prefixes and Suffixes

A Prefix is a number, letter or symbol added to the beginning of a word to change its meaning.

A Suffix is a number, letter, or symbol added to the end of the word to change its meaning.

Prefixes

Prefix	Meaning	Key Word
pre	before	preview
mid	middle	midpoint
Re	after	recharge
Un	not	unlikely
anti	against	antiperspirant
in, im, il, ir	not	impatient, illogical
en, em	Cause to	Entranced, entrenched
non	not	nonflammable
Mis	wrongly	misused
sub	Under	subordinate
over	above	overestimate
fore	before	forewarn, forecast
inter	between	intersection
semi	part or half way	semi-trailer
super	above	superintendent
trans	across	transport, transcontinental
under	Below	undercarriage
De	opposite or undo	defroster
Dis	to take away	disenfranchise
post	After	post-war
Bi	both or two	bilateral
Tri	Three	triangle
quad	Four	quadrangle

Tips for improving grammar on the B & T Officer exam

Capitalization

Capitalizing the first letter of a word indicates the word is being used in an important way. Here are guidelines which will help you capitalize correctly.

1. Capitalize the first word of a sentence and the pronoun I anywhere in the sentence.

Ex.- The department bought a motorcycle, and I learned how to ride it.

2. Capitalize the first word in a quotation.

Ex.- The victim exclaimed, "Leave me alone, I don't know who you are!"

3. Capitalize the first word and all titles and nouns in the salutation of a letter and the first word in the complimentary close.

Ex.- Dear Lieutenant Baker,
Ex.- Sincerely, Yours truly,

4. Capitalize the names of the days of the week, holidays, months of the year, historic events, and eras.

Ex.- Wednesday, Labor Day, Christmas, November, Precambrian Era.

5. Capitalize words referring to the Deity and a specific religion.

Ex.- the Creator, Judaism, Christian, Muhammad

6. Capitalize the specific names of the following:
- Geographical sites & places: Rocky Mountains Lake Superior Austin, Texas
- Regions: the Northeast, the South, the Middle East
- Organizations: the United Nations, American Red Cross, Knights of Columbus
- Buildings: Empire State Building, Chrysler Building

- Works of engineering: Eiffel Tower, Great Wall of China, Lincoln Memorial
- State abbreviations: NY, MA, WY, CA

7. Capitalize words based on nationalities or historical background.
Ex.- Texan, Floridian, Irish, Japanese, Bostonian

8. Capitalize the name brand but not the generic product's name.
Ex.- bandage, Band Aid, Ford trucks

9. Capitalize the names of your classes
Ex. Biology 101, Forensics 101, English 101.
N.B. You would not capitalize the topic of your class in a sentence such as "I do not enjoy solving geometry problems for my Math 101 homework.

Below is a list of some words that should NOT be capitalized.
trees: oak, willow
flowers: pansy, rose, dandelion
diseases/illnesses: cancer, mumps, gout
titles following a pronoun/article: my dad, our boss
seasons: fall, winter, spring, summer
directions: north, south, east, west

Capitalization Exercises
Directions: Put a line under any letter that should be capitalized. Put a slash (/) through any letter that should not be capitalized.

1. My partner Frank said, "we can't go to the Jasper Jones Community Center for the Christmas dinner."
2. There were many Laws in Roman Society.
3. If you drive South on smith street, you will arrive at county seat drive.
4. one hundred fifty years have passed since the civil war ended.
5. The james joyce festival held each summer in boston is a must for drama Students.
6. The office of judge Jones is located on the Third Floor of the Wyoming County office building.
7. The new cadets are reading "12 angry men" by Reginald Rose.
8. Marigolds and impatiens are among the first flowers to appear in City Garden.
9. The mayor will hold a news conference next Monday on the steps of City hall.
10. i recently read miller's "self-defense for police."
11. Father works at M & B bank, and Mother drives a bus for the the MTA.
12. the lusitania sank after it was struck by a Torpedo in the atlantic ocean, west of ireland.
13. This Summer i hope to drive east and visit new york, atlanta, and maybe I'll have time to go to boston to see the u.s.s. constitution.
14. "If you want work overtime," said captain morgan, "Be here at two o' clock."
15. My Doctor said that the pain in my right side was Pancreatitis, not irritable bowel syndrome.
16. The empire state building, lincoln center, and the metropolitan museum of art are all places that one should visit while in new york.
17. next quarter, i must take criminal procedure I, forensics 101, report writing, and police tactics II.

Capitalization Answer Key

1. My partner Frank said, "we can't go to the Jasper Jones Community Center for the Christmas dinner."
2. There were many laws in Roman society.
3. If you drive south on Smith Street, you will arrive at County Seat Drive.
4. One hundred fifty years have passed since the Civil War ended.
5. The James Joyce festival held each summer in Boston is a must for drama students.
6. The office of Judge Jones is located on the third floor of the Wyoming County office building.
7. The new cadets are reading "12 Angry Men" by Reginald Rose.
8. Marigolds and impatiens are among the first flowers to appear in City Garden.
9. The mayor will hold a news conference next Monday on the steps of City hall.
10. I recently read Miller's "Self-Defense for Police."
11. Father works at M & B bank, and Mother drives a bus for the the MTA.
12. The Lusitania sank after it was struck by a torpedo in the Atlantic Ocean, west of Ireland.
13. This summer I hope to drive east and visit New York, Atlanta, and maybe I'll have time to go to Boston to see the U.S.S. Constitution.
14. "If you want work overtime," said Captain Morgan, "be here at two o' clock."
15. My doctor said that the pain in my right side was pancreatitis, not irritable bowel syndrome.
16. The Empire State Building, Lincoln Center, and the Metropolitan Museum of Art are all places that one should visit while in New York.
17. Next quarter, I must take Criminal Procedure I, Forensics 101, Report Writing, and Police Tactics II.

Colons, Hyphens, Parentheses

1. A **colon (:)** is used at the end of a complete thought to introduce a list, an explanation, or a formal quotation. (Do not use a colon if the list or explanation is connected to the sentence without a complete stop.)

Ex.-To repair the cruiser, we need these parts: a fuel injector and a intake manifold gasket.

Ex.-This bullhorn is not worth repairing: the replacement parts are hard to find and it is difficult to repair.

Ex.-King's "I Have a Dream" speech begins with these words: "Five score years ago a great American in whose symbolic shadow we stand today signed the Emancipation Proclamation."

Ex.-The three students who passed the quiz were cadets Jones, Baker, and Smith. (No stop, so no colon needed.)

2. A **hyphen (-)** is used to join two or more words together that are being used to describe a noun. It is also used in some compound words and with some prefixes (all-, ex-, self-) and suffixes. It is used with numbers and to divide a word between syllables at the end of a line. Study the following examples:

Ex.-We were delayed by a slow-moving thunderstorm. The Mayor-elect was disappointed with our progress.

Ex.-Captain Biggs teachers a self-defense course to abused women.

Ex.-Every cadet was assigned to read chapters 7-9 during the break.

3. **Parentheses ( )** are used to include information that you want to de-emphasize or that wouldn't normally fit into the flow of your text but you want to include anyway.

Ex.-Chapter Seven (pages 221-256) is one of the most important we will study this semester.

Colon, Hyphen, and Parentheses Exercises

Insert **colons** as needed in the following sentences.

1. Here's what I need at the supermarket butter, apples, peanuts, and lettuce.
2. Jazz, Blues, and Bluegrass these are all types of music that is performed at the library.

B. Insert **hyphens** and **parentheses** as needed in the following sentences.

1. seven hundred people have been invited to the speech
2. Foot patrol not my favorite assignment can be a laborious detail.
3. The mayor elect of our city the son of the previous representative is an outstanding leader whom most agree will do well for Hobart.
5. Cadets at least the ones who hope to pass the examination should read pages 204 229 before Next Tuesday.
6. The First World War 1914 1919 caused great carnage and destruction, especially among people who lived near the battlefields and who had family members fighting at the front.

Colon, Hyphen, and Parentheses Exercise Answer Key
Insert **colons** as needed in the following sentences.
1. Here's what I need at the supermarket: butter, apples, peanuts, and lettuce.
2. Jazz, Blues, and Bluegrass: these are all types of music that is performed at the library.

B. Insert **hyphens** and **parentheses** as needed in the following sentences.
1. seven- hundred people have been invited to the speech
2. Foot patrol (not my favorite assignment) can be a laborious detail.
3. The mayor elect of our city (the son of the previous representative) is an outstanding leader whom most agree will do well for Hobart.
5. Cadets (at least the ones who hope to pass the examination) should read pages 204 229 before Next Tuesday.
6. The First World War 1914-1919 caused great carnage and destruction, especially among people who lived near the battlefields and who had family members fighting at the front.

Using Commas

1. Use commas to separate words, phrases, or clauses in a **list or series**. However, if all the items in the list are connected by conjunctions "or," "nor," or "and," then no commas are needed.

Ex.- The motto for the police department is courtesy, professionalism, and respect.

Ex.- Steak and eggs, fruit and granola, and oatmeal were served for breakfast.

Ex.- Frank or Pete or Jane or Rosa are assigned to the post.

Ex.- He was smart and intelligent and detailed.

2. Use a comma to separate introductory words and phrases from the sentence. For example:

After the tour was over, we went home.

Having sounded the alarm, the security guard fled.

In 1879, the Sherriff's office was established.

Yes, the police are on their way.

3. Use commas to separate interrupting words and phrases.

Ex.- Sargent Peters will, in fact, serve on the Civilian Complaint Review Board.

Ex.- Chief Williams, who was in my cadet class, appointed me to Lieutenant.

4. Use a comma with a conjunction (and, but, or, so, for, yet) to make a **compound sentence**.

Ex.- She helped me with my accident reports, and then she went to the gym.

5. Use commas in **addresses and dates**.

Ex.- The precinct is located at at 22 West Main Street, North Hollywood, California.

Ex.- She was born on December 7, 1941.

Ex.- She was born in September 1998. (comma not needed without the day)

6. Use commas with **direct quotations**. For example: "I have to study for the POST exam," my partner explained. I responded, "Good thinking."
"I wish," commented Grace, "that you wouldn't call me so early in the morning."

7. Use commas with words of **direct address**. For example: Frank, start the car. Tom, take out the door.

Comma Exercises

Provide commas as needed in the following sentences. If a sentence does not need a comma, write "N" for "No Comma Needed".

1. Because she has been working so hard in Criminal Procedure she expects to pass the class.

2. Tony has without a doubt been the most effective officer; however his partners have also proven themselves to be effective as well. Because of my illness I have not been able to make as many arrests as them.

3. I like to practice Karate work out and lift weights but what benefits me the most is jogging.

4. Frank you can send the crime scene photographs to me at 22 North Main Street North Hollywood California.

5. Sara was the highest scoring cadet because the paid attention in class studied every night and read each morning.

6. No one in my training class could handle the cruiser on the course like Charlie who had experience racing driving a truck and operating a tank in the army.

7. My favorite sergeants are the ones who make clear announcements give clear expectations and offer sound advice even when they've already given the briefing.

8. "I saw the suspect come in the front door stuffing things in his jacket as he walked to the back" said Scott the store clerk.

9. The community cleanup committee installed sprinklers planted bulbs trimmed hedges and cleaned up the park.

10. The replacement cruisers will be here next week and have all the latest sirens computers and suspension systems.

Comma Exercise Answer Key

Provide commas as needed in the following sentences. If a sentence does not need a comma, write "N" for "No Comma Needed".

1. Because she has been working so hard in Criminal Procedure, she expects to pass the class.

2. Tony has, without a doubt, been the most effective officer; however his partners have also proven themselves to be effective as well. Because of my illness, I have not been able to make as many arrests as them.

3. I like to practice Karate, work out, and lift weights, but what benefits me the most is jogging.

4. Frank, you can send the crime scene photographs to me at 22 North Main Street, North Hollywood, California.

5. Sara was the highest scoring cadet because the paid attention in class, studied every night, and read each morning.

6. No one in my training class could handle the cruiser on the course like Charlie, who had experience racing, driving a truck, and operating a tank in the army.

7. My favorite sergeants are the ones who make clear announcements, give clear expectations, and offer sound advice, even when they've already given the briefing.

8. "I saw the suspect come in the front door, stuffing things in his jacket as he walked to the back", said Scott the store clerk.

9. The community cleanup committee installed sprinklers, planted bulbs, trimmed hedges, and cleaned up the park.

10. The replacement cruisers will be here next week, and have all the latest sirens, computers, and suspension systems.

Semicolon Usage

1. Semicolons are to separate two independent clauses that are not joined by a conjunction
Ex.- The participants in the training were paid overtime; those in the second training were paid the training rate.

2. Semicolons are used to separate elements in a series that already contain commas
Ex.- The rank order was sergeant, corporal, private; private, corporal, sergeant; corporal, sergeant, lieutenant.

3. Another use (less common than the previous two) for the semicolon is to connect sentences with coordinate conjunctions (and, but, or, nor, for, so, yet) if one or more of the sentences contain a comma or commas:
Ex.- Tina wanted to be a detective; but she learned from her father, who had been a detective for many years, that to become a detective would take great effort and determination.

4. Semicolons may be used to separate items in a series when they are unusually long or contain internal punctuation.
Ex.- I am currently taking Forensics, which I find easy; Report Writing, which I find tedious; and Abnormal Psychology, which I find fascinating.
Ex.- The following people were invited: Tim, my cousin; Erik, a good friend; Sandy, a neighbor; and Francis, a colleague.

Semicolon Exercises

Directions: Add only semicolons or commas to the following sentences:

1. The confidential informant has always been accurate however sometimes I don't believe his motives.

2. Frank has been a good partner however sometimes I don't agree with his methods.

3. I am very disappointed with my running times therefore I am going to redouble my efforts tomorrow.

4. I understand the crime nevertheless I can't seem to solve who may have committed it.

5. The protestors were too violent the reverend as a result stopped speaking and left the pavilion.

6. The protestors began vandalizing the neighborhood as a result the riot team was activated and cleared the area.

8. I will talk to victim first the nurse will then give him a thorough examination.

Semicolon Exercise Answer Key
Directions: Add only semicolons or commas to the following sentences:
1. The confidential informant has always been accurate; however sometimes I don't believe his motives.
2. Frank has been a good partner; however sometimes I don't agree with his methods.
3. I am very disappointed with my running times; therefore I am going to redouble my efforts tomorrow.
4. I understand the crime; nevertheless I can't seem to solve who may have committed it.
5. The protestors were too violent; the reverend as a result, stopped speaking and left the pavilion.
6. The protestors began vandalizing the neighborhood; as a result, the riot team was activated and cleared the area.
8. I will talk to victim first; the nurse will then give him a thorough examination.

Written Expression Sample Question

NOTES: Responded to a call from 1325 Mockingbird Lane. Residence of Francine and Zachary Taylor. Parked in front of house. Saw a man on the Taylors' porch. Identified himself as Mr. Johnson, a neighbor.

QUESTION: Which one of the following choices most clearly and accurately expresses the facts presented in the notes?

A. I responded to a call from 1325 Mockingbird Lane, the residence of Francine and Zachary Taylor. When I parked in front of the house, I saw a man on their porch. He identified himself as Mr. Johnson, a neighbor.

B. Responding to a call from 1325 Mockingbird Lane, the residence of Francine and Zachary Taylor, and parking on the street in front of the house, I saw a neighbor on their porch, who identified himself as Mr. Johnson.

C. When I responded to a call from 1325 Mockingbird Lane, the residence of Francine and Zachary Taylor, I saw parking on the street in front of their house a man on their porch who identified himself as Mr. Johnson, a neighbor.

D. Responding to a call from 1325 Mockingbird Lane, I saw a man on the porch of Francine and Zachary Taylor's residence. He identified himself as Mr. Johnson's neighbor.

SOLUTION:

Choice A: This choice presents all the information in the notes in the correct sequence. This choice states that the officer responded to a call from the Taylor residence, parked in on the street in front of the house, and saw man on their porch who identified himself as Mr. Johnson, a neighbor.

Choice B: "I saw a neighbor on their porch" suggests that the officer knew that it was a neighbor on the porch before Mr. Johnson told the officer who he was. This choice is incorrect.

Choice C: This response is not phrased and punctuated correctly. This choice is incorrect.

Choice D: This choice does not identify 1325 Mockingbird Lane as the residence of Francine and Zachary Taylor Also, another piece of information is missing: the officer does not write that he parked in front of the house. This choice is incorrect.

The correct answer is A.

Grammar, Punctuation, and Spelling Question Set

Directions: The passages below each contains five numbered blanks. Read the passage once quickly to get the overall idea of the passage. Read it a second time, this time thinking of words that might fit in the blanks. Below the passage are listed sets of words numbered to match the blanks. Pick the word from each set which seems to make the most sense both in the sentence and the total paragraph.

The Secretary of State___(1)___ the county clerk of the county ___(2)___ which the commission of a notary public is filed may certify to the official character of ___(3)___ notary public and any notary public may file his autograph signature and a certificate of official character in the office of ___(4)___ county clerk of any county in the ___(5)___ and in any register's office in any county having a register and thereafter such county clerk may certify as to the official character of such notary public.

Question 1	Question 2	Question 3	Question 4	Question 5
A. that	A. in	A. all	A. any	A. State
B. of	B. at	B. many	B. all	B. town
C. your	C. for	C. such	C. none	C. village
D. or	D. to	D. all	D. neither	D. hamlet

Answers: (1.D, 2. A, 3.C, 4.A, 5.A)

The world is (1) different now. For man holds (2) his mortal hands the power to (3) all forms of human poverty and all forms of human life. And yet the same revolutionary (4) for which our forebears fought are still at issue around the globe — the belief that the rights of man come not (5) the generosity of the state, but from the hand of God.

John F. Kennedy's Inaugural Address

Question 1	Question 2	Question 3	Question 4	Question 5
A. that	A. at	A. abolish	A. beliefs	A. where
B. another	B. for	B. tell	B. kind	B. from
C. very	C. in	C. believe	C. reason	C. whether
D. a	D. behind	D. suggest	D. offer	D. with

Answers: (1. C, 2. C, 3. A, 4. A, 5.B)

When in the Course of human events (1) becomes necessary for one people to dissolve the political bands which have connected them (2) another and to assume (3) the powers of the earth, the separate and equal station to which the (4) of Nature and of Nature's God entitle them, a decent respect to the opinions (5) mankind requires that they should declare the causes which impel them to the separation.

- Declaration of Independence

Question 1	Question 2	Question 3	Question 4	Question 5
A. that	A. at	A. abolish	A. beliefs	A. of
B. another	B. with	B. among	B. Laws	B. from
C. it	C. in	C. believe	C. reason	C. whether
D. a	D. behind	D. suggest	D. offer	D. with

Answers: (1. C, 2. B, 3.B, 4. B, 5.A)

Identifying Errors in Sentences

1. The cadets <u>have learned</u> that <u>they</u> can handle problems more effectively <u>through</u> active listening <u>and not</u> through show of force.
A. have learned
B. they
C. through
D. and not
E. No Error

2. <u>After</u> hours of physical training, the commander has decided <u>to suspend</u> further training <u>of the cadet</u> until <u>their</u> next session.
A. After
B. to suspend
C. of the cadet
D. their
E. No Error

3. At the graduation ceremony, Henry <u>enjoyed listening</u> to the commissioner's insightful message, <u>which he</u> thought was <u>more sophisticated</u> <u>than the other speakers</u>.
A. enjoyed listening
B. which he
C. more sophisticated
D. than the other speakers
E. No Error.

4. Originally a <u>protest against</u> <u>stop and frisk policies</u>, the Innocence project <u>exerted</u> great influence on policing <u>of its</u> time.
A. protest against
B. stop and frisk policies
C. exerted
D. of its
E. No Error

5. <u>The officers</u> <u>made an</u> amazing arrest <u>when he</u> took <u>in three</u> bank robbery suspects.
A. The officers
B. made an
C. when he
D. in three
E. No Error

6. The <u>car ignored</u> the stop sign <u>and proceeded</u> to cross the intersection <u>and crash</u> <u>into a</u> parked garbage truck.
A. car ignored
B. and proceeded
C. and crash
D. into a
E. No Error

7. The perpetrator ran <u>through the</u> courtyard <u>and across</u> the park <u>until they</u> collapsed <u>from exhaustion</u>.
A. through the
B. and across
C. until they
D. from exhaustion
E. No Error

8. A weapon <u>must be</u> handled <u>with cares</u> and respect <u>at all</u> times. The <u>use of</u> a deadly weapon is not to be taken lightly.
A. must be
B. with cares
C. at all
D. use of
E. No Error

Answers: (1. D, 2. D, 3. D 4. E, 5. C, 6. A, 7.C, 8. B)

Memorization

This type of question is quite common on many law enforcement civil service exams. It requires you to read a passage, usually about 300-350 words, for 5 minutes. The proctors then instruct you to put the passage away, and you are given a set of 5 or so questions to answer completely from memory. The questions are very specific in nature, and many candidates who do well have trained in reading deliberately and practiced memory exercises.

In preparing this book, I gave example questions to readers of all different educational backgrounds, had them read the paragraph for 5 minutes, and administered a question set. What I found is as follows:

Most readers read through the passage in 1-1 ½ minutes. Many then read through it a second time, and said "I'm Done". They felt that they had gotten the information. When I administered the question set, they all admitted that they were not prepared to answer such specific questions.
They had not read it carefully or thoroughly.

The first lesson from this study was that a candidate must use all of the time given. Five minutes is a long time, and when used carefully, a candidate can read through the passage 3 or
Second, A watch is necessary to help the reader pace the timing.

Third, the most successful candidates used visualization strategies and ordering to help remember various details and events.

Try to imagine yourself in the place you are reading about (most likely a prison). As you read details, make mental pictures placing you in the scene you are reading about.

If an incident in the reading takes place on the 3rd floor of a 3 story building. Make a mental image of what it looks like.

If a day of the week is given, such as Tuesday, think of something you do only on Tuesdays, or think of a song with that day in the title such as "Ruby Tuesday".

If a name is given, think of somebody you know with that name, or of a famous person who shares that name.

If times are given, try to order the events from earliest to latest-then recall them in order.

After reading the material the first time, look away briefly and mentally test yourself on the details. Ask yourself the "who", "what", "when", and "where" for details in the reading.

Train yourself to recall, a paragraph at a time, the details. As you can see, it is active brain work to remember and visualize all of these details.

Train yourself to use up every second of reading time. You want to over-learn this material to the point of mastery.

There can be two types of memorization questions. The first type is a written passage and the second type is a picture.
Let's try a practice question set of a written memorization question:

You are provided with a written description of an event or incident and given a five (10) minute period to read and study the written description, after which you will turn the page and cannot look back at it. You will be instructed to not make any written notes about the event or incident. After 10 minutes you will be asked a series of questions about the facts you have read.

Directions: Read the brief story on the next page. Study it for ten minutes. Then, turn the story over and answer the five questions on the following page.

A small coffee shop is located just south of the escalator on the ground floor of the 50 Broadway. In addition to coffee and newspapers, the shop sells buns, cookies, candy, chips, soda, and assorted fruits. In the mornings between 7:00 and 11:00 A.M., donuts and bagels also are available. Employees of the building as well as tourists often purchase items there. People also stop to ask directions because the building directory is located at the main entrance of a food court, which is on the other side of the building. The coffee shop is open daily from 7:00 A.M. to 5:00 P.M. It is operated by Frank James, who is 42 years old, has brown hair, brown eyes, and a thick build. His cousin, Mary Mercer, is a single mother and helps out part time.

On the morning of Wednesday, March 2, 2005 at about 9:15 A.M., off duty MTA B & T Officer Stanley Jones stopped at the stand to purchase a bottle of water. While he was getting his water, a young man came up and asked where to find a Notary Public. He told him to take the elevator to the second floor and then turn right at the water fountain. While he was giving the directions, he noticed that Ms. Mercer was attempting to open a box of Swedish Fish candy with a box cutter.
The box cutter slipped and cut a laceration about 4 centimeters long in her right hand.
The court officer covered the wound with a sterile dressing from the first aid box, and Ms. Miller was taken to St. John's Hospital. She received fourteen stitches. Ms. Mercer did not return to work at the coffee shop for two weeks.

Examination Questions: Remembering Facts and Information

1. Who covered the wound with the sterile dressing?
A. Stanley Jones
B. Mary Mercer
C. Frank James
D. Marion Mueller

2. On what day of the week did the incident occur?
A. Monday
B. Tuesday
C. Wednesday
D. Thursday

3. The name of the hospital was
A. St. James
B. St. Johns
C. St. Alban's
D. St. Anne's

4. The Notary Public is located
A. On the 2nd floor
B. On the 3rd floor
C. On the 4th floor
D. On the 5th floor

5. What hours is the newspaper stand open?
A. 7:00 A.M. to 2:00 P.M.
B. 7:00 A.M. to 5:00 P.M.
C. 7:00 A.M. to 10:00 A.M.
D. 7:00 A.M. to 4:00 P.M.

Answers:(1. A, 2. C, 3. B, 4. A, 5. B)

Directions: Read the brief story on the next page. Study it for ten minutes. Then, turn the story over and answer the five questions on the following page.

The MTA administrative office is located in Jamaica, NY, which is in Queens County. There are three wings, a lobby and five floors. MTA Officer Francis James is one of the 33 officers assigned to this building, along with one Captain. There are generally five officers on each floor and three on patrol.

Officer James's hours are from 7:00 A.M. to 4:00 P.M. It is her 7th year as an officer and her 3rd at that location. Her first assignment was at the Cross Bay Bridge. She hopes to one day be reassigned to the Marine Park Bridge, which is closer to her home.

On Friday, February 6, 2009 Officer James is on patrol in the first-floor hallway. At approximately 10:15 A.M., Captain Mary Richards walks up to her and tells her that she needs her help on the 2nd floor. When Officer James enters G Hall, she sees two people engaged in an altercation. One woman, Ms. Lilly Peters, has her hands on the other woman's head and appears to be pulling her hair. Captain Richards grabs Ms. Peters from behind, while Officer James takes charge of the other.

Captain Richards then places Ms. Peters under arrest. Officer James asks the other person, Ms. Lisa Roberts, if she needs any assistance and she refuses. The officer then gives Ms. Peters a summons for disorderly conduct.

Captain Richards takes Ms. Peters to a waiting police car and returns to the office. She thanks Officer James for her help, commends her on her actions and instructs her to complete the appropriate paperwork. She completes the form, turns it in to the Captain for review, and clocks out at 4:15 P.M.

Questions about the story on the next page ....

Examination Questions: Remembering Facts and Information
1. What are Officer James's hours?
A. 7:00 A.M. to 4:00 P.M.
B. 11:00 A.M. to 5:00 P.M.
C. 7:00 A.M. to 5:30 P.M.
D. 11:00 A.M. to 5:30 P.M.

2. The incident takes place in what county?
A. New York
B. Richmond
C. Queens
D. Bronx

3. What is the name of the woman who was being attacked?
A. Richards
B. Blake
C. Roberts
D. James

4. How many floors are there in this building?
A. Two
B. Four
C. Five
D. Twelve

5. Who took the woman to the police car?
A. The Sergeant
B. Court Officer Johnson
C. The Lieutenant
D. Court Officer James

Answers: (1. A, 2. C, 3. C, 4. C, 5. C)

Directions: Read the brief story on the next page. Study it for ten minutes. Then, turn the story over and answer the five questions on the following page.

The Kings County Medical Detention is located on 333 Jay Street, Brooklyn NY. There are three wings, a main lobby and five floors. There are seven floors. Correction Officer Marcus Jeffries is one of the 16 officers assigned to this building, along with one Captain and one Deputy Warden. There are generally two officers in each floor and two on patrol.

Officer Jeffries' hours are from 8:00 A.M. to 5:00 P.M. It is his 7th year as a Correction Officer and his 4th at that location. His prior assignment was in the Central Booking Building in Queens County. He hopes to one day be reassigned to the The Bronx House of Detention, which is closer to his daughter's school.

On Friday, March 19, 2013 Correction Officer Jeffries' is on patrol in the 3rd floor, North Wing. At approximately 9:45 A.M., Captain Jessica Northrup walks up to him and tells him that she needs his help on the 4th floor in H Hall. When Correction Officer Jeffries enters the Hall, he sees two men engaged in an altercation. One of the men, Martin Wright, has his hands blocking his face while the other man appears to be punching him. Captain Northrup grabs the woman from behind, while Officer Jeffries takes charge of inmate Wright.

Captain Northrup then places Marcus Horn under arrest. Officer Jeffries asks inmate Wright if he needs any assistance and he requests first aid for a contusion to his head.. The officer then gives inmate Horn a summons for disorderly conduct.

Captain Northrup takes inmate Horn to a holding cell and returns to the office. She thanks Officer Jeffries for his help, commends him on his actions and instructs him to complete the appropriate paperwork. He completes the form, turns it in to the Deputy Warden for review, and clocks out at 5:30 P.M.

Questions about the story on the next page ....

Examination Questions: Remembering Facts and Information

1. What are Correction Officer Jeffries' hours?

A. 7:00 A.M. to 4:00 P.M.

B. 11:00 A.M. to 5:00 P.M.

C. 8:00 A.M. to 5:00 P.M.

D. 11:00 A.M. to 5:30 P.M.

2. The incident takes place in what county?

A. Richmond

B. New York

C. Kings

D. Queens

3. What is the name of the man who was being attacked?

A. Wright

B. Blake

C. Perkins

D. Anderson

4. How many floors are there in this building?

A. Two

B. Seven

C. Three

D. Twelve

5. Who took the man to the holding cell?

A. The Captain

B. Court Officer Johnson

C. The Deputy Warden

D. Court Officer Miles

Answers: (1. C, 2. C, 3. A, 4. B, 5. A)

Directions: Read the brief story on the next page. Study it for ten minutes. Then, turn the story over and answer the five questions on the following page.

The Queens County House of Detention building is a distinctive, Modern Classic of a building, built between 1938 and 1940. It was built with local funds combined with a grant from the Federal WPA. Mayor Stinson laid the cornerstone in 1938, and presided over the building's dedication on October 22, 1940. The building consolidated various County correctional facilities in downtown Jamaica.
The Classical style of the building was chosen as it expressed the power and majesty of the law. A classic example of the style, the E shaped seven-story building is faced with Arkansas limestone and is ornamented with neo-classical features. Its most prominent feature is a tall colonnaded entrance fronted by a grand staircase. At the center of the building the three entrances retain their original bronze doors and are edged with bronze panels depicting famous lawgivers. Other notable features include the heavy bracketed cornices, balustrade balconies, stylized swagged relief panels, and shallow window surrounds.
Architects Alfred H. Elias and William W. Golden were Queens County residents with architectural practices in Forest Hills who had designed a number of important New York City buildings. In 1940, just before it opened, the building was awarded first prize as one of the Best Buildings of the Year in New York State. The building's carefully constructed and designed facades, beautiful details, and the power of its imposing entrance make it one of finest and most awe inspiring public buildings in Queens County.
    Today, the building houses the Queens County lockup as well as prisoner holding facilities. Its visiting hours are 8:30-5:00 Monday through Friday. Central booking is located in Marvin Gardens.

Questions about the story on the next page ....

Examination Questions: Remembering Facts and Information

1. What are the visiting hours for the Queens County House of Detention?
A. 8:30 A.M. to 5:00 P.M.
B. 11:00 A.M. to 5:00 P.M.
C. 8:00 A.M. to 5:30 P.M.
D. 11:00 A.M. to 5:30 P.M.

2. Where is central booking located?
A. Kew Gardens
B. Forest Hills
C. Marvin Gardens
D. Leonia

3. What is the name of one of the building's architects?
A. Parkington
B. Blake
C. Golds
D. Elias

4. What mayor laid the cornerstone?
A. Koch
B. Giuliani
C. Bloomberg
D. Stinson

5. What is the facing of the building made of?
A. Brick
B. Concrete
C. Arkansas Limestone
D. Vermont Granite

6. What date was the building dedicated?

A. July 4, 1776   B. December 7, 1941

C. October 22, 1940   D. March 10, 1972

Answers: (1.A, 2.C, 3. D, 4. D, 5. C, 6. C)

Memorization: Picture Type Questions

Directions: Read the brief story on the next page. Study it for five minutes. Then, turn the story over and answer the five questions on the following page.
You are provided with a picture and given a ten (10) minute period to read and study the image, after which it is removed. You will be instructed to not make any written notes about the picture. You will then be asked to answer a series of questions based on the image. You will not be able to return to the image.

Study the image below for ten minutes and then turn the page to answer the questions from memory.

Questions:

1. What is the name of the church?
A. New World Church of God   B. New Life Church of God
B. New Life Church   D. New World Church

2. What time is Sunday service?
A. 8:00 A.M.   B. 9:00 A.M.
C. 11:00 A.M.   D. 12:00 A.M.

3. What time is Sunday school?
A. 8:00 A.M.   B. 9:00 A.M.
C. 11:00 A.M.   D. 12:00 A.M.

4. What is the address of the Queens Children's Health Clinic?
A. 22-01 Forest Hills St.   B. 22-01 Forest Hills Ave.
C. 22-03 Forest Hills St.   D. 22-03 Forest Hills Ave.

5. What is the phone number of the Queens Children's Health
Clinic?
A. (923)-234-6234   B. (954)-223-1918
C. (923)-231-9753   D. (932)-232-1910

6. What does the Eye Care store specialize in?
A. Glaucoma   B. Sunglasses
C. Cataracts   D. Contact Lenses

7. What is the phone number of the Dental Office?
A. (923)-234-6234   B. (954)-223-1918
C. (923)-232-1918   D. (932)-232-1910

8. How many cars are visible?
A. 0   B. 1   C. 2   D. 3

9. How many people are visible?
A. 0   B. 1   C. 2   D. 3

10. Stanley Tax Services advertises that they are
A. Fast, Reliable, Inexpensive   B. Fast, Reliable, Accurate
C. Quick, Reliable, Accurate   D. Fast, Reasonable, Accurate

11. How many windows are visible on the top floor of the building?
A. 2   B. 4   C. 6   D.

12. What is the phone number for Stanley Tax Services?
A. (923)-234-6234   B. (954)-223-1918
C. (923)-231-9753   D. (932)-232-1910

Answers:

1. B, 2. B, 3. C, 4. B, 5. C, 6. D, 7. C, 8. A, 9. A

10. B, 11. 6, 12. A

Study the image below for ten minutes and then turn the page to answer the questions from memory.

Questions:

1. What is the name of the bus company?
A. Quick Bus Co.   B. Fast Bus Co.
C. Speedy Bus Co.   D. Easy Van Co.

2. What is the name of the cross street?
A. Rockaway Blvd.   B. Rockaway Ave.
C. Rockaway Street   D. Rockaway Place

3. What is the name of the address of the Collision shop?
A. Rockaway Blvd.   B. Rockaway Ave.
C. Rockaway Street   D. Rockaway Place

4. What is the address of the collision shop?
A. 23-14   B. 22-22   C. 23-45   D. 34-56

5. What is the name of the Laundromat?
A. Quick Wash   B. QWIK Wash
C. Quick Clean   D. QWIK Clean

6. What is the shape of the Laundromat sign?
A. Octagon   B. Triangle   C. Square   D. Hexagon

7. What is the name of the sign shop?
A. ABC Sign Corp.   B. XYZ Sign Corp.
C. ABC Signs   D. XYZ Signs

8. How many buses are present in the image?
A. 0   B. 1   C. 2   D. 3

9. How many windows are visible above the sign shop?
A. 1   B. 2   C. 3   D. 4

10. How many Pedestrians are visible?
A. 0   B. 1   C. 2   D. 3

Answers: (1. C, 2. B, 3. B, 4. A, 5. C, 6. A, 7. B, 8. B, 9. 4, 10. A)

Study the image below for ten minutes and then turn the page to answer the questions from memory.

Questions:

1. What kind of Food does the restaurant sell?
A. Chinese   B. Fried Chicken   C. Lasagna   D. Pancakes

2. What kind of vehicle is present?
A. Van   B. Sedan   C. Coupe   D. Jeep

3. How much does a double cheese burger cost?
A. $6.50   B. $8.99   C. $5.50 $17.50

4. How much does a large pie cost?
A. $6.50   B. $8.99   C. $5.50 $17.50

5. How much does a 10 piece chicken cost?
A. $6.50   B. $8.99   C. $5.50 $17.50

6. 3. How much does a 15 pc. Mixed chicken cost?
A. $6.50   B. $8.99   C. $5.50   D. $17.50

7. What is the name of the restaurant?
A. ABC   B. XYZ   C. DRG   D. MRE

8. How many pedestrians are visible?
A. 0   B. 1   C. 2   D. 3

9. What is the name on the street sign?
A. Frank St.   B. Henry St.   C. Henry Ave.   D. Frank Ave.

10. What does the Graffiti say on the wall?
A. Frank Rules!   B. Henry Rules!
C. Henry Sucks!   D. Frank R.I.P.

Answers: (1. B, 2. D, 3. A, 4. C, 5. B, 6. D, 7. C, 8. A, 9. B, 10. A)

Problem Sensitivity

This is the ability to recognize or identify the existence of problems. It involves both the recognition of the problem as a whole and the parts of the problem. You will not be expected to solve the problem, only to identify or recognize the problem. Examples of this ability are recognizing when to: stop and question a group of individuals; treat an injured person; wait for medical assistance; call in information about roadway conditions; or report a mechanical issue with a squad car. This ability would also involve recognizing an explanation that someone provides in a particular situation that is diversionary or untruthful.

Strategies for Problem Sensitivity Questions
There are two types of Problem Sensitivity questions that you may encounter. The first type will begin with the presentation of some rules, procedures, or recommended practices followed by the description of an incident or situation in which these rules should be applied. Based on the applicable rules, you will be required to identify a problem (or the most serious of several problems) in the way the incident was handled. Because this first type of Problem Sensitivity question typically involves the presentation of a large amount of initial information, many of the suggested strategies for verbal comprehension questions (e.g., underlining key information) will assist you with these types of questions.

The second type of Problem Sensitivity question will consist of stories or descriptions by victims and witnesses. For these questions, a problem exists when a victim or witness gives information that is different from information supplied by other witnesses.

Problem Sensitivity Sample Question Type A
A Bridge and Tunnel Officer may have to use his or her vehicle on a roadway to warn drivers of a hazardous road condition by blocking the hazard and activating the flashing light bar.
For which one of the following should an officer place a block the roadway?
A. A 4-lane road with no emergency phone.
B. A narrow 2-lane road with an obstruction in the middle.
C. A road recently repaved.
D. A road covered with dry leaves.

Correct Answer: B.

Problem Sensitivity Sample Question Type B
A Bridge and Tunnel Officer may be called upon to help settle disputes between motorists. Which one of the following situations should the officer help settle?
A. Two men arguing about a minor traffic accident.
B. Two motorists stopped at the side of the road jumping a car.
C. Four senior officers discussing vacation schedules with a payroll coordinator.
D. A woman having a discussion with an officer about the EZ Pass program

Correct Answer: A. It is the only choice that indicates some type of conflict. Conflict can lead to violence.

Problem Sensitivity Practice Set

1. B & T Officer Davis interviewed four witnesses to an accident that took place in the tunnel approach. They described the accident as follows:

Witness 1 - "The white car caused it by swerving.."
Witness 2 - "The guy in the white car was changing lanes a lot and didn't use his signals."
Witness 3 - "the guy in the white car was racing and changing lanes. He kept moving in and out through traffic until he hit the other guy."
Witness 4 - "I was following my Cousin Francis in the white car and the other guy just crashed into him."

According to the information provided, Officer Francis should recognize that there is a problem with the account given by witness:
A. 1.
B. 2.
C. 3.
D. 4.

2. Use the information in the following passage to answer this question:

Law Enforcement Agencies have standard procedures in place for handling calls for hostage/ jumper situations:

I. Certified dispatchers attempt to keep the caller talking and work to obtain as much information possible, while working to calm the caller.

II. No attempt is made to enter the premises where the call is coming from until all units are in place and a command post is set up.

III. The decision to evacuate a building or surrounding areas is to be made by the commanding officer once the command post is established and personnel are in place.

IV. No public statements are to be made to the media by B & T Officers until the scene is secure.

V. If one perpetrator commits violence, there is always the possibility of additional perpetrators nearby are targeting law enforcement personnel. In this regard, every effort should be made to maintain a secure perimeter, and a room by room, thorough search can be made. Once the all clear signal is given, traffic can resume.

According to the preceding passage, of the four actions described below, the potentially most serious error would occur if:

A. Immediately after a hostage shooting, Sargent Thomas began shooting blindly into a bus.

B. While standing by at the scene of a hostage situation, probationary officer Jones provided information regarding the incident to a reporter.

C. While standing by at the scene of a "Jumper", Officer Smith told onlookers to move back to a safe distance.

D. After ha "Jumper" situation ended and the all clear signal was given Captain Rodriguez informed the stopped motorists they could proceed over a bridge.

3. Officer Francis is patrolling a toll plaza around 7:30 a.m. when he notices a car that is missing a rear license plate and has a loud exhaust. He pulls the car over for a traffic stop. As he steps out of the police car, the driver of the car steps out of her vehicle and walks towards him with what appears to be receipts for automotive repairs.

Before Officer Francis can say a word, the driver apologizes for the loud exhaust and explains that she had just paid a mechanic a great sum of money. She shows Officer Francis her driver's license and says that she hopes that the situation can be taken care of quickly. The woman seems frustrated and upset; she does not smell of alcohol, and she walks straight and without swaying. Officer Francis orders the woman to go back inside her car. He adds that he will also need to see proof of insurance. The woman hesitates to return to the vehicle. Officer Francis again orders the woman to return to her car. The woman states, "This isn't necessary, I am not doing anything wrong. I need to get to work or I'll be fired". Officer Francis must order her to return to her car a third time before she complies.

Based on the above information, what, if anything, is most likely to be the woman's problem?
A) The woman is just impatient to return to work.
B) The woman has something in his car that he does not want Officer Francis to see.
C) The woman is under the influence of alcohol.
D) The woman is nervous because she has no insurance, registration, or inspection and fears a ticket.

4. Officer Harley noticed a teenage girl wearing a heavyweight coat sleeping in an MTA bus shelter at 4:30 AM. Officer Harley approached the girl and asked if everything was okay. The girl stated that everything was OK, but that she was hungry. Officer Harley noticed that the girl had what appeared to be cigarette burns on her arms. She asked the girl how she received the burns, and the girl quietly replied that she had been injured baking cookies. Officer Harley was not convinced that burns were caused in the way described by the girl.

Based on the information above, what information should Officer Harley use as evidence of the girl's injuries?

A. The information regarding the girl's baking.

B. The fact that a woman reported seeing the girl.

C. The fact that the girl was wearing a heavy coat.

D. The fact that the girl did not give a plausible explanation for the injuries and got quiet when discussing their cause.

5. Imagine that you are a Bridge and Tunnel Officer assigned to supervise several people arrested during a disruptive march across an MTA bridge. Which of the following problems would you investigate FIRST?

A. A prisoner complains that another detainee in the vicinity is repeatedly humming loudly, interrupting everybody's sleep.

B. A prisoner repeatedly curses to himself.

C. A prisoner is complaining of being thirsty.

D. A prisoner informs you that another detainee in the holding area has passed out and is foaming at the mouth.

6. A Bridge and Tunnel Officer responds to the scene of an accident. Four people are injured. Which person does the officer tend to first?

A. A 24 year old man complaining of a sore hand

B. A 7 month old baby who is blue and appears to be choking

C. A 7 year old girl who is alert but crying

D. A 54 year old woman who is complaining that she bumped her head but who is and alert and talking clearly.

7. Which scene appears to be a potential problem?

A. Two women having coffee at a sidewalk café

B. 3 teenagers playing basketball in a park

C. A store owner arguing with a delivery man over an unpaid bill

D. a man walking his dog on a leash.

8. Four calls come into dispatch at the same time. Which call is the highest priority?

A. A report of a stalled car on the shoulder of a bridge approach.

B. The report of an injured bird on the embankment of a bridge.

C. A call that there is a small pothole at the approach to the toll plaza.

D. A report of an accident involving a school bus and a chemical truck.

9. A law enforcement officer has the right to search lost or abandoned property for the purpose of ensuring public safety and attempting to locate and return property to its rightful owner. Which scenario would empower an officer to search property?

A. A pocketbook found alone on a park bench with no owner visible.

B. A car parked overnight at the municipal parking garage

C. the garage of a known drug dealer

D. A vacation home that is not currently occupied.

10. You are a Bridge and Tunnel Officer. At roll call, your commanding officer gives you instructions that are unclear to you. What should you do?

A. You should respectfully ask the commanding officer to repeat the unclear instructions.

B. You should call your friend, a retired captain for assistance.

C. Follow only the parts of the instructions that you understand, and ignore the rest.

D. Complete the task as best as you can and then check with the Commanding officer if the task was done correctly.

11. **Rule:** According to the MTA rules, officers will NOT make comments to the press or make notification to the relatives of an officer who is killed or injured while on duty without the permission of the Commanding Officer.

Situation: An officer from the Queens Midtown Tunnel was seriously injured while responding to a motorist in distress. Upon returning to his post, Officer Thompson received a call from Officer Washington's wife, asking to speak to officer Washington, Officer Thompson informed her that officer Washington was at the hospital because he got injured while helping a motorist.
Officer Thompson's action was:

A. Proper, because officer Washington's wife asked for him.

B. Proper, because the family always should be notified as soon as possible in cases of serious injury or death.

C. Improper, because officer Thompson did not have the authority to make such a notification.

D. Improper, because this kind of notification should be done in person.

12. Officers are required to use handcuffs to secure detainees. When officers are using handcuffs, what action would pose a threat to the person in custody?

A. protecting the prisoners head when placing them in a squad car.

B. using a seat belt to ensure the prisoner is safe while driving.

C. tightening the handcuffs so that they cut off circulation.

D. checking the hands often for discoloration or irritation.

Answers:

(1. D, 2. A, 3. D, 4. D, 5. D, 6. B, 7. C, 8. D, 9. A, 10. A, 11. C, 12. C)

Deductive Reasoning

Deductive reasoning begins with a general fact and creates a specific conclusion from that generalization. This is the opposite of inductive reasoning, which involves creating broad generalizations from specific observations. The basic idea of deductive reasoning is that if something is true of a group of things, this truth applies to all members of that group. One of the keys for successful deductive reasoning, then, is to be able to correctly identify members of the group, because incorrect categorizations will result in incorrect conclusions. For deductive reasoning to work, the original fact must also must be correct. If the original fact is wrong, even if the logic used is correct, the answer will still be wrong.

You can better understand deductive reasoning by looking at an example. A generalization might be something such as, "Every Octopus has eight arms." A logical conclusion for this example is, "This is an Octopus, so it must have eight arms." This is a valid deduction. The truth of the deduction, however, depends on whether the creature is actually an octopus. A common error in this logic would be to say "This creature has eight arms, so it must be an octopus".

On the exam you will be asked how to apply general rules to particular cases. There are two different types of deductive reasoning questions which appear on law enforcement exams:

1. Applying rules and procedures to particular situations
2. Applying legal definitions to the facts of particular situations.

Applying Rules and Procedures

In constructing law enforcement exams, test makers treat department rules and procedures as general principles which must be applied in the circumstances of particular situations. Questions based on rules or procedures begin with a statement of the department rule or procedure. For example, the question could state the procedure for signing in before roll call. The question might then give a description of an officer arriving to work late. The question will then ask about how the officer should go about signing in.

When answering these questions, do not think about your own experience. You may be familiar with the policy or procedure being tested. Do not let this cloud your reasoning. Everything you need to know to answer the question is contained in the policy or procedure provided.

Rules and procedures assure that laws are enforced fairly and equally, allow for a chain of command to operate, and enhance the ability of various law enforcement and public safety agencies to coordinate a response to an emergency. These questions are designed to test your ability to follow and apply a rule. There will not be any "trick" psychological questions in this part.

Here are some strategies for answering deductive reasoning questions:

1. Follow the steps of a procedure in order.

2. Pay attention to when the rule is in effect.

3. Pay attention to when the rule is not in effect.

4. Identify when there are exemptions to a rule and know when to apply the exemption. The key words to help you identify an exemption are "unless", "except", "when", and "if".

5. If a rule or procedure has several parts, make sure the answer satisfies all of the parts. When answering this type of question, it is important for you to reread the question and ask yourself, "is there anything missing from this answer?"

6. In choosing an answer, apply rules exactly as written. Remember, this is an exam for an entry level position in law enforcement. The exam is testing how well you follow directions and carry out orders, not how well you interpret vague philosophy.

Applying Legal Definitions

This exam requires the candidate to apply laws to situations. The test-taker is not expected to know any of the laws. The laws are stated as part of the question. These questions look like reading comprehension questions, but they are designed to test the candidate's ability to reason based on legal definitions and apply them to specific situations. These questions provide the definitions for several different classes of crimes. the definitions are oversimplified. Your task for answering this type of question is to answer the question based solely on the definition provided and not from your own background knowledge.

After providing several definitions, the questions describe a specific situation. The candidate is then asked what type of crime, if any, was committed and who committed it.

These questions require you to pay careful attention to detail. You can count on there being answer choices that are in place to catch up a careless or fast reader.

The definition of a crime will have several parts, all of which must be present for a crime to have taken place. If any one of the parts is missing, then the particular crime could not have been committed.

Try to break the definition down into its parts. Make a mental checklist. In order for the crime to have been committed, all parts of the checklist must be satisfied.

While reading a legal definition, be on the lookout for important punctuation marks like colons or semicolons that may be indicators of the separate parts of a definition. Also watch out for the words "and" and "or". Use of the word "and", means that two or more parts must have occurred for a crime to have been committed. If the word "or" is used, then only one part out of many is necessary for the crime to have been committed.

Strategies for answering Deductive Reasoning Questions

1. Read carefully. There are false choices designed to catch up a careless reader.

2. Make sure the choice matches all parts of a rule, policy, or definition.

3. Use only the information provided. Do not rely on your own knowledge of an actual rule or definition.

4. Keep in mind that these questions are meant to test your ability to follow directions. Your job is not to interpret how correct a policy or definition is.

Sample Question Applying Rules and Procedures

RULE: Patrol vehicles should be inspected immediately prior to the start of each shift. Do not assume that the vehicle is in safe working condition. Check that all of the lighting is operational, all emergency equipment is present, operate the siren, check engine, oil level, engine coolant level, gasoline level, tire pressure and condition, spare tire, lug wrench, jack, windshield wipers and windshield washer fluid level. Check the body of the vehicle for damaged or missing parts and report any damage or malfunction to your sergeant. At the end of your shift, leave the vehicle in safe operational condition for use by the next officer.

SITUATION: Officer Davis is about to begin his patrol shift when he discovers that his Transportation Van has a large scratch and dent in the right rear quarter panel. He knows that the vehicle did not have this dent yesterday, when he last drove it.

QUESTION: According to the above Rule, Officer Davis should most properly

A. request that he be assigned a different vehicle

B. begin his shift and be alert to any operating problems

C. find out what other officers have used the vehicle since his last shift

D. inform his sergeant about the dented bumper

SOLUTION: The Situation states that Officer Davis has discovered a dent in the quarter panel of his patrol vehicle that did not exist when he last used it. The question asks what he should do about it. To answer the question, evaluate all of the choices.

Choice A states that the officer should request a different vehicle. There is nothing in the rule that states that the officer should do this. Choice A is incorrect.

Choice B states that the officer should begin his shift and be alert to any operating problems. The rule states that the officer should report any problems with the vehicle to his supervisor. Choice B is correct.

Choice C states that the officer should find out what other officers have used the vehicle since his last shift. There is nothing in the rule that states that the officer should do this. Choice C is incorrect.

Choice D states that the officer should inform his supervisor about the damaged quarter panel. This conforms to the given rule that states that the officer should report any problems, damage, or discrepancies to her supervisor. Choice D is the correct answer.

The answer is D.

Rule Relating to Leaves of Absence

Prepare Leave of Absence Report and submit to commanding officer for approval, at least five days before leave commences except in emergency.

2. Leaves may be terminated at discretion of the Commissioner.

3. Member who is granted extended leave of absence without pay must take all accrued leave prior to the start of leave of absence, except for military leave.

4. Leave without pay for thirty (30) or more consecutive days during a year, except military leave, will reduce authorized vacation by 1/12th for each thirty (30) consecutive days of absence.

5. Member returning from leave without pay for one (1) year or more may not be granted un-accrued vacation until member performs active duty for a minimum of three (3) months, unless otherwise authorized by law.

6. A member of the service (uniformed or civilian) applying for any extended leave, e.g., educational leave with or without pay, hardship leave, etc., is required to communicate with the Military and Extended Leave Desk for instructions.

7. Leave without pay may be granted to observe a religious holiday. No more than 1/6th of each squad may be granted such leave.

Questions:

1. If an Officer has a documented family emergency and desires to submit for a leave of absence, what must he or she do?
A. Wait five days and then submit the paperwork.
B. Go to family and apply after the fact.
C. Submit paperwork immediately requesting immediate leave .
D. Submit paperwork and wait the required 5 days.

2. If a Officer has been approved for a leave for educational purposes and an emergency strikes the City of New York, who has the power to terminate Leaves of Absence?
A. The Commissioner
B. Each commanding officer
C. The Mayor
D. No one. The Leave was already granted.

3. If a member is called up for military service.
A. He must first use up all of his accrued leave time.
B. He does not have to use his accrued leave time.
C. He must not go.
D. He must wait until a replacement is found.

4. A member goes on Leave without pay for 31 days. She has accrued 12 vacation days. How many days will be deducted?
A. 12
B. 6
C. 3
D. 1

5. A member returns from a two your leave of absence. How long must he or she wait until they may apply for a vacation?
A. Immediately
B. 1 month
C. 3 months
D. 1 year

6. A member desires to take a leave of absence to attend law school at Brooklyn Law. With whom must the member communicate with?
A. Desk Sargent
B. Commanding Officer
C. Internal Investigations desk
D. Military and Extended Leaves Desk

7. A Squad has 60 members. The Easter Religious Holiday is approaching. How many members may be granted an unpaid leave of absence from the squad?
A. None B. 6   C. 10   D. 60

Answers: (1. C, 2. A, 3. B, 4. D, 5. C, 6. D, 7. C)

PROCEDURES for Utilizing the Information System

Purpose:

To inform members of the service of the guidelines to be complied with when accessing, creating, receiving, disclosing or otherwise maintaining information from an information system:

1. Access only those information systems to which authorization has been granted, and under circumstances required in the execution of lawful duty.

2. Abide by any security terms/conditions associated with the information system, including those governing user passwords, logon procedures, etc. All users must log out any time they leave the terminal.

3. Disclose information to others, including other members of service, only as required in the execution of lawful duty.

4. Confirm identity and affiliation of requestor of information and determine that release of information is lawful, prior to disclosure.

5. Maintain confidentiality of information accessed, created, received, disclosed or otherwise maintained during course of duty.

Questions:

1. If an officer desires to use the system, when is it permissible to borrow another officer's password?

A. During off-duty hours

B. During regular shift

C. Never. Access is not authorized

D. Only with cooperating officer present

2. An officer is using the information system terminal and feels the urge to use the restroom. The officer should

A. logoff

B. turn off screen

C. Ask Sargent to watch computer

D. leave it on, as it will take too long to reboot

3. An officer has a friend that works for a local newspaper. The friend requests information from the officer. The officer should
A. arrest the friend
B. refer the friend to the office of media relations
C. allow the friend to only view the material, not print it.
D. print the information the friend requested

4. What should an officer do if someone calls on the office phone and states that they are with the FBI and need information about the deployment of department resources to high risk areas?
A. Offer to give the information
B. Hang up
C. Refer the caller to the commanding officer for verification of credentials
D. Take down the caller's information and then give them the requested information.

Answers: (1. C, 2. A, 3. B, 4. C)

UNIFORMS

1. Maintain at own expense articles prescribed for rank, position or duty. Cadets wear uniform only after inspected and stamped by MTA Academy.
2. Do not modify prescribed uniforms in any manner except as specifically authorized by higher authority.
3. Do not wear distinguishable items of the uniform with civilian clothes.
4. Do not wear uniform, shield or display **IDENTIFICATION CARD** while participating in a rally, demonstration or other public assemblage except as authorized by the Department.
5. Wear uniform of the day. Commanding officers or unit commanders may authorize a specialized uniform only after requesting and receiving approval from the Commissioner's Uniform and Equipment Review Committee. Submit requests to the Office of the Chief of Department: Att: Uniform and Equipment Sub-Committee.
a. Wear uniform when directed, if assigned to the administrative Bureau or to duty in civilian clothes.
6. While performing duty indoors, in uniform, wear regulation seasonal shirt and trousers.
7. Wear the prescribed uniform, if regularly assigned to duty in uniform, when appearing in court, the Trial Room or at the office of a ranking officer above the rank of captain, except if off duty, on sick report, or if excused by competent authority.
8. Purchase regulation service holsters, caps, raingear and all items of uniform which are sewn or attached to the uniform, from the Equipment Section or other authorized supplier.
9. Necessary uniform changes, other than those listed in step 10, will be made as directed by the lieutenant platoon commander/counterpart.
a. The lieutenant platoon commander/counterpart shall authorize the removal, if desired, of the duty jacket/summer blouse whenever the temperature for a **specific** tour is expected to rise above 65 degrees Fahrenheit.
b. The lieutenant platoon commander/counterpart shall authorize the wearing of the **optional** short sleeve shirt whenever the temperature for a **specific** tour is expected to rise above 70 degrees Fahrenheit.

Questions:

1. An officer desires to replace uniform articles. He or she must
A. Submit a voucher for payment from the department
B. Request the new articles from the Quartermaster at 75-20 Astoria Ave. East Elmhurst, N.Y.
C. Pay for the articles from an authorized vendor
D. Wait until the annual uniform fund is established.

2. An officer desires to place a small gold cross on the left collar of the uniform. Who may authorize such an alteration?
A. The Commissioner's Uniform and Equipment Review Committee
B. The Union
C. The officer's Clergy
D. Fellow officers

3. An officer desires to attend an immigration rally. They must
A. Hand in their gun and shield
B. not wear their shield or ID card.
C. not attend any rally.
D. may proudly display badge as long as Class A uniform is worn.

4. When appearing in court, officers should wear
A. street clothes
B. regular uniform
C. Suit and tie for men, dress and blouse for ladies
D. former military uniform if ever in service

5. From who may an officer purchase a holster?
A. Any sporting goods store
B. from an authorized retailer
C. from the Academy
D. from retired officer

6. The temperature is expected to rise to 68 degrees Fahrenheit for a specific tour. The Lieutenant may authorize
A. Shorts
B. Removal of duty jacket or summer blouse
C. street clothes
D. sneakers, socks, and athletic wear

7. The temperature is expected to rise to 80 degrees Fahrenheit. The Lieutenant may authorize the use of
A. shorts
B. short- sleeved shirt
C. Sneakers
D. Street clothes

Answers: (1. C, 2. A, 3. B, 4. B, 5. B, 6. B, 7. B)

Rule

The Counterterrorism Bureau recently distributed personal protective equipment to over 1200 to enhance the personal safety of uniformed members in the event of a disaster or catastrophic incident, including those of a chemical or biological nature. Included in the personal protective kit is a tactical response hood contained in a cloth carry pouch. This item is designed to be attached to the gun belt worn by uniformed members. As such, it should be carried by, and available to, all uniformed members performing patrol duty in uniform.

Members are reminded that the tactical response hood is designed for a single escape of up to 15 minutes from a contaminated area. They do not provide oxygen, and are not intended for use in an oxygen-deprived environment.

2. Therefore, effective immediately, uniformed members of the service will carry the tactical response hood as follows:

a. Members performing patrol duties in a Department vehicle will have the hood and pouch available in the vehicle;

b. Members performing foot patrol duties and/or assigned to a detail such as a march or running event, fixed post, etc. will carry the tactical response hood by attaching the pouch to their gun belts on the side opposite which the member carries his/her firearm;

c. Members performing administrative or other duties inside a Department facility will have the tactical response hood and pouch readily available at all times.

3. The balance of the personal protective equipment issued to uniformed members of the service will be carried in Department vehicles by those members of the service performing patrol duties in such vehicles. All other uniformed members of the service will have the balance of the personal protective equipment readily available, e.g. stored in their Department locker.

4. Any provisions of the Department Manual or other Department directive in conflict with the contents of this order are suspended.

Questions:

1. An officer is assigned foot patrol of the Cross Bay Bridge in southern Queens, she should
A. wear the personal protective equipment
B. Carry the personal protective equipment on the gun belt on opposite side from weapon
C. Give the personal protective equipment to family
D. Leave the personal protective equipment in the trunk of the squad car

2. In the event of a chemical attack, the hood is designed to protect an officer
A. for a shift
B. for 15 minutes
C. for 1 hour
D. indefinitely

3. An officer is designed to foot patrol during the marathon. Where should the officer keep the personal protective gear?
A. In a backpack
B. In the precinct
C. At the command post
D. on their gun belt

4. A member is assigned to light duty at the precinct following an automobile accident while on duty. The officer
A. Must wear their personal protective device on their gun belt
B. must keep the personal protective device in their locker
C. does not need the personal protective device
D. Must keep the personal protective device close at hand

Answers: (1. B, 2. B, 3. D, 4. D)

Inductive Reasoning

This type of question involves combining separate pieces of data or information, to form general rules or conclusions. It requires the ability to come up with possible reasons for why things fit together.

You will be asked to make general conclusions based on the information provided in tables, charts, and graphs. Most Inductive Reasoning questions will start with a passage which provides you with the information you will need to answer the question. Scan the passage to determine the main idea, and then read the questions. The questions will ask you to identify similarities and differences within the reading. You can expect to be asked to identify trends and patterns and to predict future results based on given data.

How Improve your Inductive Reasoning Skills
Be sure to carefully read every part of the charts or graphs provided and every part of the answer options. If you misread a number or a variable, you will not be able to find the correct answer. Modern exams account for this by providing wrong answer choices that match a hastily made conclusion.

You can prepare for inductive reasoning questions by looking through a newspaper or a magazine for a chart or graph. Before reading the article or advertisement that accompanies the graph, try making your own interpretations and conclusions about the data. Then read the article to see if your conclusion matches the analysis given by the text.

Many advertisements use graphs to "spin" their product. Try to identify ways that a graph or chart is misleading. Analyze charts and graphs for missing information that changes the meaning.

Sample Question

During a simulation exercise, cadets at the Academy learn that as officers, they may have cause to secure scenes containing the remains of a deceased person. In this instance, an immediate notification must be made to the desk officer of the precinct of occurrence, so that the medical examiner can send a team to the scene. Due to the nature of the situation and the possibility that a crime has been committed, ALL members of the MTA B & T Division will follow these guidelines:

1. Do Not disturb personal affects.
2. DO NOT make jokes or remarks concerning the condition of the body.
3. DO NOT take pictures with the deceased
4. Use your nose. If chemical vapors are very strong or there is any odor of bitter almonds, remain outside and call for HAZ Mat response.
5. DO NOT disturb the body.
6. DO NOT talk to the press
7. DO NOT provide personal information to neighbors or onlookers.

Based on this information, it would be most correct for the cadets to conclude that the primary concern behind these guidelines is:

A) Proper control of evidence at a possible crime scene until a search warrant can be obtained.

B) Safety of the officers concerning possible explosions or exposure to fumes.

C) Keeping officers from accidental or intentional exposure to controlled substances (e.g. narcotics).

D) Preservation of professional and safe scene concerning the nature of the situation.

The correct answer is D.

Crime Statistics

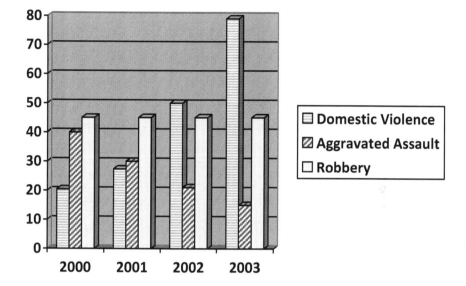

1. According to the graph, Robbery
A. Increased   B. Fluctuated
C. Decreased   D. Remained the same

2. Which crime had the most instances in any given year?
A. Domestic Violence   B. Aggravated Assault
C. Robbery   D. All were equal

3. Which crime increased each year?
A. Domestic Violence   B. Aggravated Assault
C. Robbery   D. All remained stable

4. Which crime declined each year?
A. Domestic Violence   B. Aggravated Assault
C. Robbery   D. All decreased each year

5. Which crime had the lowest incidents in 2002?
A. Domestic Violence   B. Aggravated Assault
C. Robbery   D. Robbery and Domestic

6. Which year had the lowest crime overall?
A. 2000   B. 2002
C. 2001   D. 2003

7. If current trends continue, predict what will happen to the number of Aggravated Assault cases.
A. It will increase   B. It will decrease
C. It will remain stable   D. It will fluctuate

8. If current trends continue, predict what will happen to the number of domestic violence cases.
A. It will increase   B. It will decrease
C. It will remain stable   D. It will fluctuate

Answers: (1. D, 2. A, 3. A, 4. B, 5. B, 6. C, 7. B, 8. A

Causes of Accidents 2013

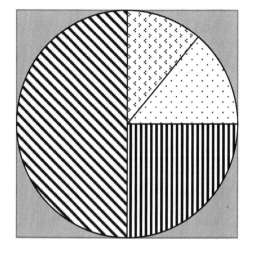

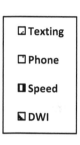

- ☑ Texting
- ☐ Phone
- ◼ Speed
- ◥ DWI

1. According to the graph, what is the greatest cause of accidents?
A. Texting   B. Phone   C. Speed   D. DWI

2. What is the approximate percentage of DWI accidents?
A. 100%   B. 75%   C. 50%   D. 25%

3. Which cause is about 25%?
A. Texting   B. Phone   C. Speed   D. DWI

4. Phones and Texting together cause as many accidents as
A. Texting and Speed   B. Phones and Speed
C. Speed   D. DWI

5. According to the graph, what is the lowest cause of accidents?
A. Texting   B. Phone   C. Speed   D. DWI

6. Which cause of accidents is greater than phone but less than DWI?

A. Texting   B. Phone   C. Speed   D. DWI

7. Approximately what percentage do Speed, Texting, and Phone Cause combined?

A. 25%   B. 50%   C. 75%   D. 100%

8. Approximately what percentage of accidents does Speed cause?

A. 25%   B. 50%   C. 75%   D. 100%

Answers: (1. D, 2. C, 3. C, 4. C, 5. A, 6. C, 7. B, 8. A)

Precinct Calls by Type and Year

	2010	2011	2012	2013
Car Accident	11	17	18	22
Auto Theft	15	21	17	19
Robbery	22	29	38	42
Petty Larceny	99	102	118	120
Total	147	169	191	203

1. According to the table, which year had the highest number of incidents?
A. 2010   B. 2011   C. 2012   D. 2013

2. According to the table, which incident happens the most often?
A. Car Accident   B. Auto Theft
C. Robbery   D. Petty Larceny

3. According to the table, which incident happens the least often?
A. Car Accident   B. Auto Theft
C. Robbery   D. Petty Larceny

4. According to the chart, precinct calls are
A. Increasing   B. Decreasing   C. Remaining stable

5. According to the chart, which incident occurs more often than Robbery?
A. Car Accidents   B. Auto Theft
C. Petty Larceny   D. Murder

6. According to the table, which incident fluctuates?

A. Car Accident   B. Auto Theft

C. Robbery   D. Petty Larceny

7. According to the table, which incident occurred less than Auto Theft in 2011?

A. Car Accident   B. Burglary

C. Robbery   D. Petty Larceny

8. Predict which type of call will increase the least in 2014

A. Car Accident   B. Auto Theft

C. Robbery   D. Petty Larceny

Answers: (1. D, 2. D, 3. A, 4. A, 5. C, 6. B, 7. A, 8.B)

Information ordering

This type of question requires following a set of rules or actions in a certain order. The rules will be given. The things or actions to be put in order can include numbers, letters, words, or sentences. Questions based on information ordering measure your ability to put information into a logical order. You might be given sentences which will have to go into a paragraph, and then you are instructed to create the paragraph. You might be given a group of items and you will have to classify them. You might be asked to list things in chronological order according to time.

For information ordering questions, it is often best to come up with the answer before you look at the answer choices. After you read the information and the question, imagine the correct answer. Then look at the answer choices to find your answer. In this way, you will be verifying your answer.

Typically, it will be easy to determine the first and last items in the set. You can then eliminate the choices which clearly aren't correct and can then use that time to locate and verify the correct choice. Some information ordering questions will provide you with a specific rule or procedure to follow. It is necessary to read very carefully, as the procedure will spell out exactly what you have to do. In this case, you can count on the test-makers to provide incorrect answer choices to catch careless reading. For example, if the question states that you must put the names in order of last name, first name, and middle initial, it would be an error to include the full middle name if given.

Some information ordering questions work in reverse. You will be given a procedure in the correct sequence with all of the steps outlined. You will then be asked questions about the ordering of the steps and will have to fit actions into the outlined procedure. Again, it is very important that you rely solely on the outlined procedure. DO not rely on your own experience for what the right order is.

The secret to success in answering information ordering questions is to be very strict in your thinking. Do not rely on outside experience.

These questions are based on the following rules :

There is only one correct order of things.

Every step must be followed in the correct stated order.

No step may be missed or omitted.

The most difficult information ordering questions include exceptions or "if", or "unless". For example, a procedure might state that an officer must use a special form if an accident she responds to will likely result in a fatality, unless the person has already been taken to a hospital. It would be an error to use the special form in all accident cases. It would also be an error to use the form if the patient has already been transported to the hospital. Therefore, it is important to take note of any time the works "if" or "unless" are used or if there are any exceptions to a procedure given.

Strategies for answering information ordering questions

1. Follow the directions very carefully. Make sure you understand the task. Re-read until you are certain of what is being asked.

2. Find out what the first step is, and quickly eliminate those choices which don't fit.

3. The most difficult information ordering questions contain the words "if" and "unless". Be on the lookout for any question that includes exceptions to a stated procedure.

Sample Question

Cadet Officers in the Academy are told that if they are in a situation in which persons are being held hostage or barricaded persons will not voluntarily surrender, they should do the following in the order given:

1. Notify the Communications Division of the situation, so they can notify the Patrol supervisor, Emergency Service Unit, and Operations Unit.
2. Verify that the patrol supervisor and Emergency Service Unit are responding.
3. Attempt to confine and isolate the subjects involved, pending arrival of the patrol supervisor and Emergency Service Unit.
4. Maintain firearms control and establish CO lines.
5. Maintain continuous surveillance of the location, if possible. Detain witnesses for later debriefing.

In a role-play exercise in class, the cadet officers are given a situation in which officers respond to a barricaded person situation. They have notified the Communications Division, and have verified that the patrol supervisor and the Emergency Service Unit are responding. The next step they should take is to:
A) Direct the Operations Unit to respond.
B) Attempt to confine and isolate the subjects involved.
C) Maintain firearms control and establish
D) Detain witnesses for later debriefing.

Correct answer: B.

Information Ordering Question Set

1. Use the information in the following passage to answer the question:

When responding to an incident involving a person needing medical assistance, law enforcement officers should follow these steps in the order given:

I. Render aid to the sick or injured person.

II. Request ambulance if necessary

III. Notify the Dispatcher if the person is wearing a Medic-Alert bracelet or if a family member or acquaintance indicates that the person suffers from serious medical problems.

IV. Wait to direct the ambulance to the scene.

V. Make a second call in 15 minutes if the ambulance does not arrive.

VI. Make a Log book entry, including the name of the person notified regarding the Medic-Alert emblem or statements from family acquaintance concerning nature of illness.

While on off duty, CO Humphry is approached by a man who informs the CO that an middle aged woman has was found slumped behind the steering wheel of a car. CO Humphrey, while offering aid, notices that the woman is wearing a Medic-Alert emblem indicating Diabetes. Officer Humphrey now requests an ambulance to respond. The next step the officer should take is to:

A. inform the Dispatcher of the Medic-Alert emblem.

B. have a responsible person direct the ambulance to the scene.

C. place a second call for the ambulance after 15 minutes.

D. take the woman to the hospital in the patrol car.

2. Officer Stone has just finished interviewing the victim of an robbery.

The victim made the following statements:

1. When walking to the station, I saw my brother's friend, Charles Mason standing at the entrance.

2. Charles hit me in the face and body with repeated blows with his fist.

3. I didn't want to walk past Charles because I knew he was desperate for money to buy drugs with.

4. Charles grabbed at my backpack and attempted to run away.

5. I ran up the stairs and escaped.

6. A bus driver heard me scream and he yelled at Charles who ran away.

What is the most logical order of these statements?

A) 6, 1, 3, 5, 4, 2

B) 2, 4, 5, 3, 1, 6

C) 1, 3, 4, 2, 6, 5

D) 4, 3, 5, 2, 6, 1

3. Officer Alexander has just finished interviewing the victim of an armed bank robbery.

The victim made the following statements:

1. While working as a Teller at Steward Savings and Loan, I noticed Frank Jones on line. He looked nervous.

2. Frank Jones ran out of the bank with a brown bag full of money.

3. Frank Jones produced a note demanding money and displayed a shiny pistol

4. I showed up to work at 8:30 that morning.

5. After Frank Jones left, we closed the bank and called the police.

6. I saw Frank Jones hanging around the bank before we opened that morning.

What is the most logical order of these statements?

A) 6, 1, 3, 5, 4, 2
B) 2, 4, 5, 3, 1, 6
C) 1, 3, 4, 5, 2, 6
D) 4, 6, 1, 3, 2, 5

4. You are a Bridge & Tunnel Officer assigned to the Queens Midtown Tunnel. Your commanding officer has just distributed a laminated card with instructions for cardiopulmonary resuscitation. The instructions on the card include the following five statements:

I. After contacting emergency medical personnel, position the victim. To open the person's airway, turn him or her on his or her back, supporting the head and neck.

II. Before performing mouth-to-mouth breathing, look, listen and feel for respiratory movement.

III. To ascertain if someone requires CPR, gently shake the shoulder of the person who collapsed and shout, "Are you okay?" If there is no response begin chest compressions.

IV. When performing chest compressions, press hard, fast, and deep at a rate of at least 100 beats per minute.

V. If the person does not respond, call 911 before performing CPR.

If you place the above statements in the most logical order, which step should be performed immediately AFTER shaking, tapping or talking to the victim to ascertain if he or she requires CPR, assuming that the person needs further help?

A) Begin Chest Compressions
B) You should call 911.
C) You should position the victim on their back.
D) You should feel for a pulse.

The process for signing in to work is as follows:

I. All officers must report to the precinct 30 minutes prior to the beginning of their tour.

II. All officers must sign in at the front desk with the desk sergeant.

III. Officers may then get dressed in their official uniform.

IV. Officers must report to roll call no later than 15 minutes prior to the beginning of their tour for inspection.

V. After inspection, all officers assemble in the Ready Room where the Sergeant will brief the officers for the tour.

VI. At the exact minute the tour begins, the officers will be dismissed to begin their tour.

VII. Any lateness must be reported immediately to the desk sergeant.

5. After reporting to the precinct, the officer must first

A. assemble for inspection
B. sign in with the desk sergeant
C. get dressed in official uniform
D. go to the ready room

6. An officer reports to roll call 13 minutes before the start of their tour. What must they do first?
A. Get dressed
B. Report for inspection
C. Report lateness to desk Sergeant
D. continue and report lateness after roll call

7. After briefing, what occurs?

A. The officers put on official uniform

B. The officers sign in

C. The officers are inspected

D. The officers are dismissed

If an individual has no heartbeat or pulse, an MTA Bridge & Tunnel Officer should first remove the victim from the mechanism of injury and then initiate CPR (cardiopulmonary resuscitation). Once a victim's heartbeat and breathing are restored, other injuries can be treated. Degrees of seriousness in descending order are bleeding wounds, shock and broken bones. Minor cuts and abrasions would, of course, have the lowest priority.

8. Of the conditions listed below, which would be the one that should be treated last?

a) Deep bleeding wound

b) Heart failure

c) Sprained ankle

d) Shock

e) Minor cuts

9. Determine the order in which you would treat the injuries described above.

a) e, b, c, a, c

b) b, a, d, c, e

c) c, b, d, a, e,

d) a, b, e, d, c

e) d, a, b, e, c

The order of procedure for signing out a tow truck is as follows:

I. Request a vehicle from the fleet supervisor

II. Examine the exterior of the vehicle for visible damage. If any is noted, inform the fleet supervisor immediately.

III. Check the oil, washer fluid, transmission fluid, and brake fluid. Note any deficiencies to the mechanic in charge.

IV. Check the tires for visible damage and check the pressure. If the pressure is below 35 psi, the officer must add air to the tires.

V. Once checked, the officer must sign the vehicle out of the lot.

10. After checking the tires for damage, what should the officer do next?

A Check oil
B. Sign out vehicle from lot
C. Check washer fluid
D. Check tire pressure

11. After requesting a vehicle from the fleet supervisor, what should the officer do next?

A. Examine the exterior
B. Check brakes
C. Check tire pressure
D. Sign vehicle out

12. If an officer checks the tire pressure, and it reads 36 psi, what should they do next?

A. let some of the air out

B. Check the oil
C. Check for damage to the tires
D. Sign the vehicle out of the lot

13. If an officer checks the oil and finds it to be low, what should that officer do next?

A. notify the fleet supervisor
B. add oil
C. Notify mechanic in charge
D. take another vehicle

14. If an officer is checking the exterior of a vehicle and notes a large dent on the driver's side, the officer should

A. locate the last officer to use the car and make them report it.
B. take the car and report it after the shift
C. Find another vehicle
D. Notify the fleet supervisor

Answers:
1.A, 2. C, 3. D, 4. A, 5. B, 6. C, 7. D, 8. E
9. B, 10. D, 11. A, 12. D, 13. C, 14. D

Mathematics
Arithmetic

In this section of the exam you will be provided with situations that require the use of basic arithmetic. You will read each situation and solve the problem. You are not allowed to use a calculator in this section; scratch paper will be provided in the test booklet to do all of your figuring. There is no penalty for guessing. Your score will be the percentage of problems you answer correctly. Therefore, you should try to answer each problem.

Number Facility

Number facility is the ability to complete numerical operations including addition, subtraction, division, multiplication, decimals, percent, and fractions. This section also tests the speed and accuracy of computation.

Some Key Terms to assist you with Number Facility questions

Ratio: a comparison of two quantities by division

Proportion: two equal ratios

Percent: A ratio that compares a quantity to 100.

Scale: a comparison of one size to another using a defined measurement. Example ¼" = 1 foot.

Decimal: A placeholder that separates whole numbers from fractional points.

Numerator: The top number of a fraction

Denominator: The bottom number of a fraction.

Decimals and fractions are used to show parts of a whole number. To express any fraction as a decimal, divide the numerator by the denominator.

For example:

½ becomes .5

¼ becomes .25

To help prepare for Number facility questions, take some time to carefully complete the chart of some of the more familiar decimals, fractions, and percent.

Decimal	Fraction	Percent
.5		
	1/5	
		25%
.01		
	1/3	
		12.5%
	2.5/1	
	1/10	
1		

Conversion chart answer set

Decimal	Fraction	Percent
.5	½	50%
.2	1/5	20%
.25	1/4	25%
.01	1/100	1%
.33	1/3	33.33%
.125	1/8	12.5%
2.5	2.5/1	250%
.1	1/10	10%
1	1/1	100%

To improve your skills with working with fractions and decimals, take some time each day to work through several mixed fraction and decimal problems that you create on your own. The set below is an example:

1 ½ + 2/3 =

1.75 – 1/2=

2.33 + 2/3=

1.75 * 2.5=

Complete these questions on scrap paper by hand. Show all of your work and then check your work with a calculator. As you get more experience, use more difficult fractions such as 1/ 12 times 2/5. You will find that, given a little practice, you will become very good at these types of problems.

A Ratio is a comparison of two quantities by division. For example if a vendor always receives 2 boxes of oranges for every 3 boxes of apples we would say his ratio of oranges to apples is 2:3. A proportion is two equal ratios. If we expand on the ratio above, we could easily determine how many boxes of apples the vendor receives if he receives 4 boxes of oranges. He would receive 6.

Find the equivalent fractions that will make these ratios into proportions:

1. _____ : 3 = 18:6

2. 1 to 2 = 3 to _____

3. 4 to 2 = 20 to _____

4. 8/10 = _____ / 100

5. 22/ 11 = 30/ _____

Sample Questions

Please use the following information to calculate the correct answers to sample questions.

1. A department van has an average range of 420 miles on a full tank of gas. The gauge reads one quarter (3/4) of a tank. How far will the van be able to drive?

A. 105 miles

B. 210 miles

C. 315 miles

D. 400 miles

2. Sargent Smith needs to measure the rectangular visitor room. She uses a measuring tape to find the South wall is 18 feet and the East wall is 15 feet. What is the area of the visitor room?

A. 270 sq. ft.

B. 360 sq. ft.

C. 180 sq. ft.

D. 90 sq. ft.

Answers:

1. C

2. A

Number Facility Practice Questions

1. 22 X 11=

A. 242

B. 133

C. 2211

D. 222

2. 575/ 5=

A. 131

B. 2525

C. 250

D. 115

3. If an officer works 8 hours on Monday, 8 hours on Tuesday, 16 hours on Wednesday, 16 Hours on Thursday, and 8 hours on Friday, how many hours did he work that week?

A. 56

B. 66

C. 54

D. 46

4. An officer's rate of pay is $40.00 an hour. She earns time and a half for overtime and works 20 hours of overtime in a given week. What would her overtime be?

A. $800

B. $1,000

C. $1,200

D. $1,600

5. An cadet has $100 in his bank account. He purchases twenty chocolate bars at $0.50 per piece. He also purchases 16 packs of tuna fish at $1.50 per pack. How much will the cadet have left in his account?

A. $56

B. $66

C. $36

D. $34

6. A cadet completes 150 pushups a day for 30 days. How many pushups did she complete in total?

A. 450

B. 4500

C. 1500

D. 350

7. Rules require that there are 3 sergeants for every 25 officers. Currently there are 2025 Officers at a large city police force. How many supervisors are required?

A. 243

B. 2430

C. 234

D. 2340

8. A typist must have 25 Sq. feet of space in a cubicle. There are 10 typists in the division headquarters. How much space is required?

A. 25

B. 200

C. 250

D. 220

9. A trainee arrives at the program weighing 180 pounds. After a month, he now weighs 162 pounds. What percentage of weight did the trainee lose?

A. 5%

B. 10%

C. 15%

D. 20%

10. A Captain can retire at 20 years with a pension of 50% of her final salary. Supervisors then accrue an additional 2% per year. If a Captain works for 30 years, what percentage of her final salary will her pension be?

A. 55%

B. 60%

C. 70%

D. 80%

Answers: 1. A, 2. D, 3. A, 4. C, 5. D, 6. B, 7. A, 8. C, 9. B, 10. C

Mathematical Reasoning

Mathematical reasoning is the ability to reason abstractly using quantitative concepts and symbols. It encompasses reasoning through mathematical problems in order to determine appropriate operations that can be performed to solve them. It also includes the understanding or structuring of mathematical problems. In a sense, these are word problems.

Sample Questions

Please use the following information to answer sample questions.

When responding to an incident, the Active Incident Response Team must adjust its number of responders to the number of vehicles involved in the incident. The table below shows the suggested number of responders needed to respond to a fight.

Number of vehicles	Number of responders required
3	4
6	8
9	12
12	16

A. As the number of vehicles involved in a incident increases, the number of responders required on the scene triples.

B. As the number of vehicles involved in a incident increases, the number of responders required on the scene decreases.

C. The number of responders required on the scene increases at the same rate as the number of vehicles involved in the incident.

D. As the number of vehicles involved in an incident increases, the number of responders required on the scene also increases at a constant rate.

Correct Answer is D. For every 3 vehicles involved in an incident, four responders are required to respond.

In an attempt to reduce injuries from hazardous materials incidents, the Department has instituted a study to determine the correct number of HazMat trained officers. The table below shows the results of the investigation.

Which statement below most accurately reflects the results of the investigation?

HazMat Trained Officers	Number of Injuries from HazMat
5 officers	25
7 officers	20
9 officers	15
11 officers	10
13 officers	5

A. For every two HazMat officers added to patrol, the number of injuries decreased by 5.

B. As the number of HazMat officers increased, the number of injuries decreased proportionately.

C. As the number of HazMat officers was increased, the number of injuries increased at a constant rate and then leveled off.

D. For every two HazMat officers added to patrol, the number of injuries was cut in half.

The correct answer is A. For each two HazMat officers added, the number of injuries dropped by 5.

Mathematical Reasoning Practice Set

1. Jones is twice as old as his friend Frank. Frank is 5 years older than Ortiz. In 5 years, Jones will be three times as old as Ortiz. How old is Jones?

A. 8 years old

B. 12 years old

C. 14 years old

D. 10 years old

2. Marcus' dad is 4 times older than Marcus and Marcus is twice as old as his sister Gina. In three years, the sum of their ages will be 42. How old is Marcus now?

A. 6 years old

B. 7 years old

C. 8 years old

D. 9 years old

3. Michael scored 67, 77, 81, 75, and 82 in his Mathematical Reasoning exams. What will be his average grade in Mathematical Reasoning from this exam?

A. 77.2

B. 76.4

C. 78.1

D. 75.5

4. Roberta left work and drove at the rate of 35 miles per hour for 2 hours. She stopped for breakfast then drove for another 2 hours at 55 mph to reach training in Albany. How many miles did Roberta drive to reach Albany?

A. 110 miles

B. 70 miles

C. 90 miles

D. 180 miles

5. Diamond went to Quartermaster Supply, Inc. She bought a new duty belt and a pair of Class "A" uniform shoes. She paid $88.00 discounted for 20% off. What was the original price of the shoes?

A. $105.60

B. $66.00

C. $102.00

D. $108.00

6. If Sapphire's weekly income doubled she would be making $60 a week more than Jamie. Sapphire's weekly income is $80 more than half of Francis's. Francis makes $400 a week. How much does Jamie make?

A. $160

B. $400

C. $550

D. $500

7. A conference with 2000 participants gathers in the Bronx. One out of every five people attending the conference who have ordered meals requested Kosher. 25% of those attending the conference signed up for meals. How many requested Kosher?

A. 150

B. 125

C. 100

D. 200

8. There is a uniform allowance of $180 per officer for every six months. At this same rate, what would the uniform allowance be for 10 officers for a period of 12 months??

A. $1800

B. $2800

C. $2700

D. $3600

9. In October, The Department spent $88000, or 20% of its personnel expenses that month on overtime. What were its total personnel expenses for October?

A. $44,000

B. $880,000

C. $440,000

D. $4,400,000

10. Officer Caldwell bought an equal number of $12.00, $8.00, and $6.00 duty socks for his uniform. He spent $130 for all of the socks. How many of each did he buy?

A. 7

B. 9

C. 5

D. Cannot be determined from information given

11. Lieutenant Milton conducts foot patrols at three large housing facilities every week, except for his three-week vacation, how many housing facilities does he patrol in one year?
A. 49
B. 98
C. 147
D. 150
E. 166

Questions 12 and 13 are based on the following information.
In preparing a report of damaged equipment, officer Jones noted the following:
Snow Shovels $810
Laptop computer $650
Patrol Scooter $325
Patrol Bicycle $125

12. What was the total value of all the damaged goods?
A. $1800
B. $1810
C. $1860
D. $1910
E. $2010

13. What was the value of all the damaged goods EXCEPT the snow shovels?
A. $1100
B. $1260
C. $1585
D. $1685
E. $1785

14. During one 5-day period, officer Fernandez drove his squad car 225 miles. If he drove 85 miles on one day, how many miles did he average on each of the other days?
A. 28 miles
B. 35 miles
C. 40 miles
D. 70 miles
E. 140 miles

15. Vandals broke into a fleet of maintenance trucks and left with 30 global navigation systems with a total retail value of $6,750. What is the average retail value of each navigation system?
A. $225
B. $250
C. $275
D. $325
E. $350

16. It costs $360 for a precinct's service contract with a copier company to service 3 copiers for one year. At this rate, how much would it cost the precinct to service 9 copiers for nine months?
A. $1080   B. $720   C. $490   D. $810

17. In September, a precinct spent $6600, or 25% of its non-personnel expenses that month, for equipment repair. What were its total non-personnel expenses for September?
A. $26,400   B. $26,000   C. $33,200   D. $6,600

18. Dwayne bought an equal number of $25.00, $36.00, and $44.00 tickets for a baseball game. He spent $315 for all of the tickets. How many of each did he buy?
A. 2 B. 3 C. 4 D. 5

19. A municipality employs 3,800 people. Of these, 72% are male, and 50% of the males are age 35 or younger. How many males are there in the municipality who are older than 35?
A. 1425   B. 2850 C. 7250   D. 5072

20. A machine can process 240 250 pound containers in 28 days. If it continues to process at this same rate, how many 250 pound containers can it process in 35 days?
A. 250   C. 500   B. 320   D. 300

21. A laptop and a tablet cost a total of $1600. If the laptop cost $440 more than the tablet how much did the tablet cost?
A. $480   B. $440   C. $580   D. $680

22. A maintenance worker has a round piece of chain 1/4" in diameter and 4 yards long. She needs half the length to secure a drum and the remaining piece for 12" straps. How many straps will she have?
A. 2   B. 4   C. 6   D. 8

23. Robin can sweep a block in four hours, Susan can sweep the same block in six hours.
How long will it take them to sweep the block if they work together?
A. 4 hours   B. 2.5 hours   C. 5 hours   D. 6 hours

24. Frank and June jog 4 miles each morning. If they run at a constant rate and it takes Frank 45 minutes while June finishes in an hour, how much distance does June have left when Frank finishes?
A. 1 mile   B. 2/3 mile   C. ½ mile   D. 1 ½ miles

25. If one of every five probationary officers are women, approximately what percent of a class of 450 officers are women?
A. 6   B. 14   C. 81   D. 20

26. A custodian combines ingredients x, y and z in a ratio of 1:1:4 to produce a cleaning solution for the polisher. How many gallons of the second ingredient, ingredient y, is needed to make a 12 gallon tank of the cleaner?
A. 1 gallon   B. 2 gallons   C. 3 gallons   D. 4 gallons

27. A police department served 450,000 people in 2013. If the department served 495,000 people in 2014, this reflected an increase of:
A. 5% B. 10% C. 15% D. 20%

28. The number of officers attending a weekly training program in the month of April averaged 220 officers. If there were 200 officers attending the first week, 240 the second, and 260 the third, how many people attended the fourth week?
A. 200 B. 220 C. 240 D. 180

29. It takes 15 officers 10 days to complete a project. How long would it take 10 officers, if they worked at the same rate, to complete the same project?
A. 10 days B. 7.5 days C. 15 days D. 30 days

30. If the sum of two numbers is 400, and their ratio is 3:2, then the smaller number is:
A. 160 B. 240 C. 360 D. 400

31. The population of Queens in 2014 is 120% of its population in 2004. The population in 2004 was 2 million. What was the population in 2014?
A. 1.8million B. 2.2 million
C. 2.8 million D. 2.4 million

32. An industrial safety supply store advertises that they sell all gloves and boots at cost plus 10%. If Henry buys a pair of boots for $110, what is the stores markup?
A. $10.00 B. $45.00 C. $60.00 D. $15.00

33. A semi-trailer travels 60 miles an hour, and a squad car travels .5 miles in a minute. How far will the semi-trailer travel in the same time a squad car travels 180 miles?
A. 180 B. 240 C. 360 D. 480

34. In a Police Academy training class there are 80 students. The student-faculty ratio is 16:1. How many faculty are there for this class?
A. 4   B. 5   C. 8   D. 16

35. From 4 p.m. until midnight, the temperature dropped at a constant rate. From midnight until 2 a.m., it dropped 3°. If at 4 p.m., the temperature was 64°and by 2 a.m., it was 37°, what was the temperature at 10 p.m.?
A. 56   B. 44   C. 46   D. 48

36. A probationary officer spends 35 hours a week in a squad car and 5 hours a week on foot patrol. What percentage of the time is he on foot patrol?
A. 10%   B. 12.5%   C. 15%   D. 25%

37. ¼ of a tank of diesel has been used. The remainder of the fuel is divided among three Emergency Service trucks. Approximately what percentage of the diesel does each truck get?
A. 12.5%   B. 25%   C. 35%   D. 75%

38. On a promotional exam a police officer scored 144 on a scale of 0-180. Her score converted to a percentage is:
A. 80%   B. 82%   C. 78%   D. 88%

39. A police officer earned $2000 during a two week period. How much would she earn during a ten week period?
A. $4000   B. $16000   C. $10000   D. $22000

40. If Jake can complete 12 accident reports in 8 hours, and Arthur can install 12 accident reports in 12 hours, approximately how many reports could both of them install in 8 hours working together?
A. 12   B. 16   C. 20   D. 24

41. A patrol car travels 20 miles when an ESU truck travels 12 miles. How many miles will the squad car travel when the ESU Truck travels 36 miles?
A. 40   B. 60   C. 30   D. 60

42. A dumpster holds 20 cubic yards of refuse. If it is 20% full, how many cubic yards of refuse can still be added to it?
A. 8 B. 16   C. 18   D. 22

43. A copy machine has used up 75% of its service life. It currently has 1000 hours left of service life. What was its original service life when new?
A. $1000   B. 2000   C. 4000   D. 40000

44. If there are 20 squad cars assigned to a district and 4 of them are out of service, what percentage of squad cars are in service??
A. 75%   B. 80%   C. 20%   D. 25%

45. A storage yard is 100 feet by 400 feet. A fence is built around the yard, at a cost of $7.50 per running foot of fencing. What was the cost of the fencing?
A. $2200   B. 7500   C. $750   D. 75000

46. A police officer earns three times as much in February as in each of the other months. What part of her entire year's earnings does she earn in February?
A. 3/14   B. 36   C. 4/12   D. 3/13

Answers: 1. D, 2. A, 3. B, 4. D, 5. A, 6. D, 7. C, 8. D, 9. C, 10.C, 11. C, 12. D, 13. A, 14. B, 15. A, 18. B, 19. A, 20. D, 21. C, 22. C, 23. B, 24. A, 25. D, 26. B, 27. B, 28. D, 29. C, 30. A, 31. D, 32. A, 33. C, 34. B, 35. A, 36. B, 37. B, 38. A, 39. C, 40. C, 41. D, 42. B, 43. C, 44. B, 45. B, 46. A

Spatial Orientation

Spatial orientation questions measure your ability to know your position or the position of an object in relation to a map or diagram, or a passage of text. For most of these questions, you will be given maps or diagrams and asked to answer questions based on them. Spatial orientation questions tend to emphasize determining your location or how to go from one place to another on the diagram or map. The most challenging spatial orientation questions are based on directions given in a paragraph of text and do not include a map or diagram. For example, the question may say that a person walked south three blocks, then turned west for two blocks, then turned north for one block, and then walked west one more block. With this type of question, it is helpful to trace the route on the desk with your finger.. This is the best way to guarantee the accuracy of your answer choice.

Many diagrams or maps use symbols and provide a key for the symbols. For instance, a note at the top or bottom of a diagram might indicate that an octagon represents a stop sign; an arrow may indicate what direction a one way street goes. Be sure to look for a key to symbols. Another important feature of many maps is the compass rose. It provides the directions for North, South, East, and West. You may need to determine East, South, and West when only given an arrow facing North.

Often questions are based on phrases like "turn right," "on your left," or "to your right," or "to the right of the front door." With this type of question, make sure you confirm which side of the image is right or left. It may not be the same as your "left" or your "right". (This is why people use the terms "port" and "starboard" in boating.)

When you are trying answer choices on this type of question, try each one only up to the point where it proves to be false. Then move on to the next choice.

Strategies for answering Spatial Orientation Questions

1. Study the key to make sure you understand symbols used for direction and the flow of traffic on a map.

2. Make sure you understand which part of the map is North, South, East, and West. (North may not always be up!)

3. If given a verbal question, do your best to visualize the scene. Place yourself in the scene described.

4. Only try choices until they are proven incorrect, then move on to the next choice.

Spatial Orientation Sample Question

In questioning a carjacking victim, you are told the suspect pulled out a knife and told "me to give me all your money". Then he ran down the block with his back to me heading westbound. He then made a left turn and ran two more blocks and then made a right turn.

According to this information, you would be most correct to radio that the perpetrator was last seen traveling:

A) North B) South C) East D) West

Answer: (D) West. The perpetrator was initially running west. He made a left turn, so he was then running south. Finally, he made a right turn and was now running west.

Spatial Orientation Question Set

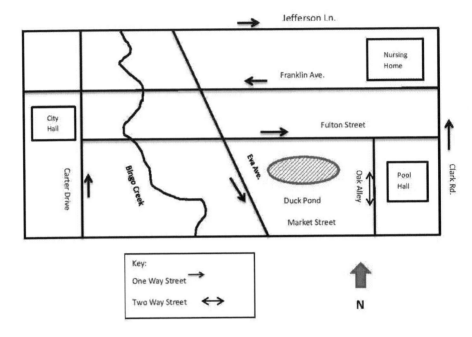

The above maps shows the downtown area. The entrance to City Hall is on Carter Drive. The entrance to the Nursing Home is on Franklin Ave. The entrance to the Pool Hall is on Oak Alley.

1. Which direction does Jefferson Ln. run?
A. East   B. South   C. North   D. West

2. City hall is located _____of the pool hall?
A. East   B. South   C. North   D. West

3. What street follows the same basic direction of Bingo Creek?
A. Carter Drive   B. Eva Ave   C. Market Street   D. Oak Alley

4. What is the shortest route from City hall to the Pool Hall?
A. Carter Drive to Market Street   B. Fulton Street to Oak Alley
B. Franklin Ave. to Carter Drive   D. Bingo creek to Market St.

5. What is the shortest route from the pool hall to the nursing home?

_____

6. What direction is Duck Pond from the intersection of Fulton Street and Bingo Creek?
A. East   B. South   C. North   D. West

7. What direction does Eva Ave. run?

_____

Answers:
1. A
2. A
3. B
4. B
5. Oak Alley, Fulton Street, Clark Road, and Franklin Ave.
6. A
7. Southeast

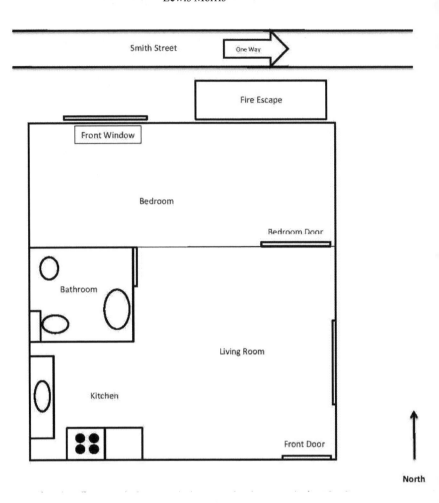

1. If an officer is on the fire escape looking in, in what direction is the front door?
A. North   B. South   C. East   D. West

2. If a resident is looking out the living room window, what direction are they looking? _____

3. What direction does Smith Street run?
A. North   B. South   C. East   D. West

4. If an officer is entering the front door, what direction must she turn to get to the kitchen?

A. Left   B. Right   C. North   D. Straight

5. If a resident is standing on the fire escape with their back to smith street, which direction are they facing?

A. North   B. South   C. East   D. West

6. If an officer is standing in the kitchen facing a fire on the stove, which direction is the front door?

A. Behind and to the right B. Behind and to the left

C. forward   D. Straight back

7. If an officer is responding to a person in distress in the bathroom, which direction would the officer go once entering the apartment?

A. forward and to the left B. Forward and to the right

C. Left   D. Right

8. If an officer can look in a window and see a person standing at the stove, from what direction is the officer looking from?

A. North   B. South   C. East   D. West

9. If an adjacent apartment shares a wall with the kitchen and is a mirror layout of the apartment shown, what direction would a person be facing if they are looking out the bathroom door?

A. North   B. South   C. East   D. West

10. If an adjacent apartment shares a wall with the kitchen and is a mirror layout of the apartment shown, what direction does the fire escape face?

A. North   B. South   C. East   D. West

11. If an adjacent apartment shares a wall with the kitchen and is a mirror layout of the apartment shown, what direction does the living room window face?
A. North   B. South   C. East   D. West

Answers:
1. B
2. East
3. C
4. A
5. B
6. B
7. A
8. C
9. D
10. B
11. D

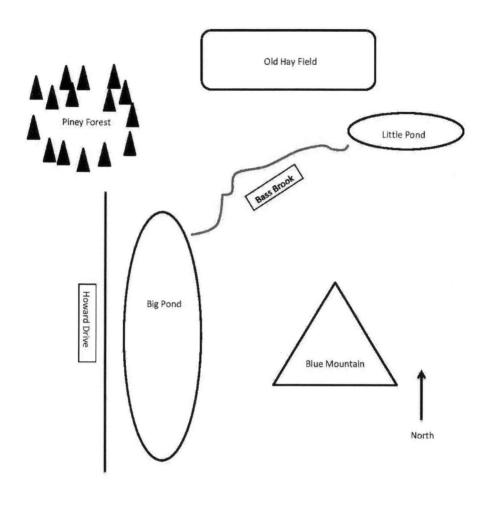

1. Which direction does Howard drive run?
A. North-South   B. East-West
C. Around   D. Diagonal

2. Which direction is it from Blue Mountain to Little Pond?
A. North   B. South   C. East   D. South-West

3. To go from Little Pond to Big Pond, which direction must you travel?
A. North   B. South   C. East   D. South-West

4. Which Direction is the Piney Forest from the Little Pond?
A. North   B. South   C. East   D. West

5. If you walked from the Big Pond along the Bass Brook toward the Little Pond, what would you see on your right?
A. Howard Drive   B. Piney Forest
C. Blue Mountain   D. Old Hay Field

6. Big pond is _____ of the Piney Forest.
A. North-East   B. South-West
C. North-West   D. South-East

7. If you are driving North on Howard Drive towards Piney Forest, Big Pond is to your
A. West   B. South   C. Left   D. Right

Answers: (1. A, 2. A, 3. D, 4. C, 5. C, 6. D, 7. D)

Visualization

This type of question requires forming mental images of what objects look like after they have been changed or transformed in some way. For example, if a convertible car were seen leaving the scene of an accident, the test-taker would be given the task of to visualizing what this car would look like with the top up. In the same way, the person with this ability would be able to visualize what a suspect would look like with a hat, sunglasses, different clothing, or different types of facial hair (see examples below).

Techniques: As shown in the example below, some of the visualization questions will consist of a drawing or photo of a face followed by a line-up of four other faces. One of these other faces is the original face in disguise. You must see through the disguise and pick out the original face.

When responding to these questions, follow these suggestions:

1. Focus your attention on unchanging parts of the face. Ignore changing parts, such as hair or changes in facial expression. The parts of the face least likely to change are the nose and the eyes. The hair is the feature most likely to be changed, including beards and mustaches, but a change in hair also can make the mouth, chin, and shape of face look different.

2. When possible, focus on parts of the face which are most influenced by the shape of the bones. The same face may be fat or thin, depending on gain or loss of weight. However, bones do not change much. For example, pay attention to shape of the chin and cheek bones when they are visible.

3. Make point-by-point comparisons between the original face and the disguised faces. Do not try to judge the face as a whole. Rule out false figures one by one on the basis of specific details.

Sample Questions
Answer questions 1 through 3 solely on the basis of the following passage.

Police Officers James and Williams are dispatched to 23-24 Camp Boulevard, Apt. D-8, at 2:34 P.M., on October 15, 2013, in response to a burglary reported by a Mr. Patterson. They arrive at the apartment at 2:39 P.M., ring the buzzer and are greeted by Mr. and Mrs. Patterson. Mr. Patterson tells the officers that he left for his job as an x-ray tech at a doctor's office at 8:00 A.M. and that his wife left for her dental assistant's job 10 minutes later. After work, Mr. Patterson picked up his wife and they returned to their apartment at 2:30 P.M. When Mrs. Patterson entered the bedroom, she noticed her jewelry box on counter opened and empty. She yelled for her husband, who then called the police. While the Patterson's waited for the police to arrive, they discovered that all of Mrs. Patterson's jewelry and Mr. Patterson's tools, as well as approximately $1,200 in cash, were stolen.

While Officer James begins to fill out a crime report, Officer Williams goes to other apartments on the floor to interview neighbors who might have seen or heard something related to the burglary.

Mrs. Stevens, age 49, a security guard, who lives in Apt. D-9 located directly opposite the garbage chute, tells Officer Williams that she heard noise in the hallway outside her apartment door at 1:15 P.M.

She thought that the voices were those of the plumbers who sometimes who had been working in an access panel in the hallway. She looked through her peep hole and saw two strange males standing by the elevator. They wore green work clothes. She noticed that the taller man was Hispanic, about 25 years old, 5'11", 210 lbs., with black hair and was carrying a red toolbox. The other man was Caucasian, about 27 years old, 5'8", 175 lbs., with black hair and a large tattoo on his left arm.

Officer Williams then contacts other residents at apartment D-5, D-6, and D-7. All of them tell the officer that they did not see or hear anything unusual. Officer Williams then returns to the Patterson's apartment to tell his partner what he learned. In the meantime, Mr. Patterson had told Officer James that his tools were in a red toolbox.

Officer James was also told that Mr. Patterson is 51 years old. His telephone number at work is (718)945-2929 and his work address is 125 Eastern Parkway. Mrs. Patterson's telephone number at work is (212)845-5161 and her work address is 223 Nostrand Ave. The Patterson's home telephone number is (718)233-2424. Mrs. Johnston's telephone number at home is (718)631-9141.

Officers James and Williams finish their investigation and complete the crime report.

1. Which one of the following was not stolen during the burglary of the Patterson's apartment?
A. $1200
B. Mrs. Patterson's jewelry
C. Mr. Patterson's toolbox
D. Credit cards

2. What is the approximate age of the taller of the two strangers seen standing near the
elevator?
A. 25
B. 27
C. 30
D. 21

3. Which one of the following identifying marks is part of the description of the shorter male
stranger seen standing near the elevator?
A. Scar
B. Tattoo
C. Birthmark
D. Mole

4. Which apartment was directly opposite the garbage chute?
A. D-5
B. D-9
C. D-2
D. D-8

Answers (1. D, 2. A, 3. B, 4)

Visualization Practice Question Set

1.

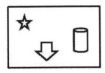

Which one of the images below represents the above image rotated clockwise 90 degrees?

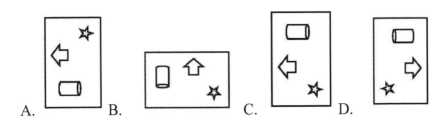

A.   B.   C.   D.

2.

Which one of the images below represents the above image Flipped Horizontally?

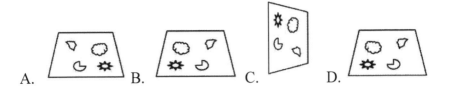

A.   B.   C.   D.

3.

Which one of the images below represents the above image flipped vertically?

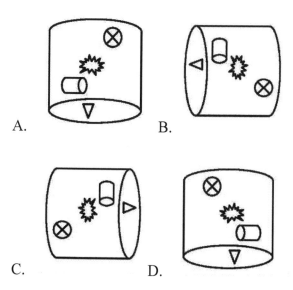

A.

B.

C.

D.

4.

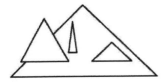

Which one of the images below represents the above image rotated 90 degrees clockwise and then flipped horizontally?

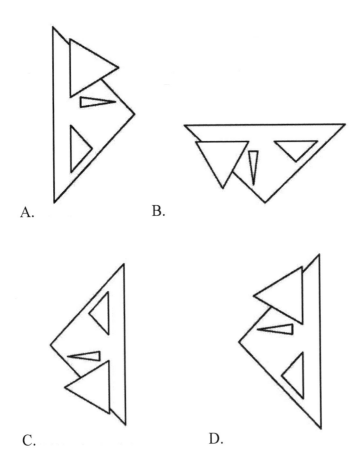

A.   B.

C.   D.

5.

Which image represents the above image flipped horizontally?

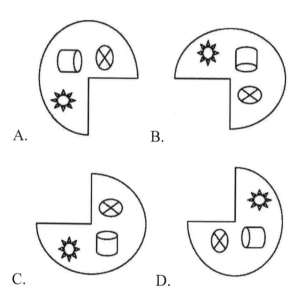

A.

B.

C.

D.

6.

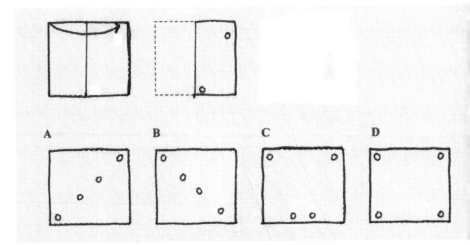

7.

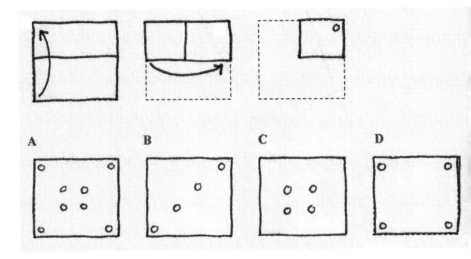

8.

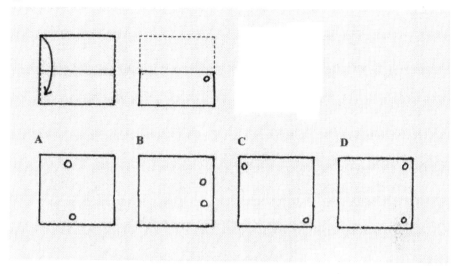

9.

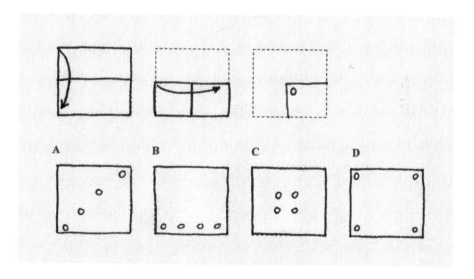

Answers: (1. A, 2. A, 3. A, 4. D, 5. C, 6. C, 7. D, 8. C, 9. C)

Glossary

Accessory: One who is not the chief actor in the offense, nor present at its performance, but is in some way involved, either before or after the act committed. One who aids, abets, commands, or counsels another in the commission of a crime. Synonym for "accomplice" or "abettor."

Admission: Generally, confessions, concessions or voluntary acknowledgments made by a person of the existence of certain facts. In the criminal context, a statement by a person of facts which in connection with proof of other facts or circumstances, tends to prove guilt, but which is, of itself, insufficient to merit conviction.

Aggravation (offense; e.g. aggravated assault, aggravated battery): Any circumstance attending the commission of a crime which increases its guilt or enormity or adds to its injurious consequences, but which is above and beyond the essential constituents of the crime itself.

Arrest: To take a person into custody, by authority of law, for the purpose of charging him/her with a criminal offense.

Arrest Warrant: A written order issued by a judge that directs a law enforcement officer to arrest a person and bring them to court.

Arson: Burning or attempting to a burn a building owned by another, with the intent to kill or seriously injury a person.

Assault: An attempt or threat to inflict bodily injury upon another, along with the apparent ability to do so, which places the victim in fear of injury or bodily harm.

Attempted Robbery: A crime that results in no property taken but the suspect is still sought for the actions leading to the attempt.

Back Up: Police officers who assist the first responders.

Battery: Battery is causing bodily harm to a person by any means, or making physical contact with a person of an insulting or provocative nature.

Bench Warrant: A document issued by the court to mandate the appearance of an individual before the court.

Blood Alcohol Concentration (BAC): The concentration of alcohol in the bloodstream.

Breathalyzer: An instrument used by trained operators to measure the Blood Alcohol Content (BAC) of a person's breath.

Burglary: Entering a dwelling, room, or building of another with the intent to carry away items or fixtures from the premises.

Carjacking: Knowingly or recklessly by force or violence, taking or attempting to take from another person immediate actual possession of the person's motor vehicle.

Child: A person who has not yet attained the age of 16 years.

Citation: An order issued by the police requiring a person to appear on a specific day and do something therein mentioned

Civil Action: A lawsuit to redress a private wrong, in which the remedies are money damages and/or injunctions.

Coercion: The threat or use of mental or physical means to get information.

Community Stakeholders: All individuals and organizations that have a vested interest in a safe and healthy community. This includes public and private institutions, social service providers, schools, churches, businesses, property owners, renters, and others.

Complainant: The victim, the arresting officer, or the person or agency filing a complaint.

Complaint: A statement under oath whereby a witness accuses an individual of criminal behavior.

Confession: A person's admissions of enough facts to establish his or her guilt of a particular crime.

Conspiracy: Agreement with another, or others, to commit a crime, and an act by any party to the agreement in furtherance of the agreement.

Contempt: An act that constitutes a violation of a court order or disrespect toward the judge or the court proceedings.

Controlled Substance: A drug or substance regulated by federal or District of Columbia law, including opiates and hashish.

Court: A tribunal having authority under the Constitution to settle disputes.

Court Appointed Attorney: An attorney appointed to represent an indigent defendant or other indigent litigant.

Crime Triangle: A tool used in problem-solving. The sides of the triangle – victims, offenders, and the location – represent the three elements of every crime situation. The crime triangle is used in problem solving to foster a thorough analysis of crime patterns and more effective actions that will reduce the harm caused by a problem.

Criminal Action: A lawsuit in which the state or the public, rather than a private party, is plaintiff, and the defendant faces punishment such as a fine or incarceration if convicted.

D.O.A.: Abbreviation for "dead on arrival" as applied to a person who expires before reaching a medical facility.

D.O.B.: Abbreviation for "date of birth."

Delinquent: A person under the age of 18 who has been adjudicated for an act that would be a crime if committed by an adult, and who requires guidance treatment, and rehabilitation.

Detective: A sworn member of the Department responsible for the follow-up investigation of crime.

Disorderly Conduct: An act which unreasonably alarms or disturbs another and provokes as breach of the peace.

Distribution of a Controlled Substance: Knowingly and intentionally transferring or attempting to transfer a controlled substance to another person.

Driving Under the Influence: Driving while intoxicated with alcohol.

Duress: Forcible restraint or restriction.

Evidence: Oral statements, documents, sound and video recordings, and objects admissible in court. To be admissible, evidence must be material (it must go to a substantial issue in the case) and relevant (it must go to the truth or falsity of a matter asserted).

Extradition: The surrender by one state to another of an individual accused or convicted of an offense outside its own territory and within the territorial jurisdiction of the other, which being competent to try and punish him, demands the surrender.

Felony: An offense for which a sentence of death or a term of imprisonment for one year or more is provided.

Field Sobriety Test: Tests of coordination given at the time and on the scene of a traffic stop to assist in determining if an individual is intoxicated.

Frisk: A limited protective search for concealed weapons and/ or dangerous instruments. Usually it occurs during a "stop" and consists of a pat down of the individual's clothing to determine the presence of weapons or other dangerous objects. An officer may frisk a person on the basis of "reasonable suspicion" that the person is carrying a concealed weapon or dangerous instrument.

HAZMAT: Short for Hazardous Materials. A training and response protocol for dealing with chemical spills and other incidents where chemicals or dangerous materials may pose a threat to the public and responders. May also include dangerous biological or pathogenic material as well.

Homicide: The unlawful killing of a human being, including murder and manslaughter.

Homicide, Justifiable: A homicide based on the perpetrator's reasonable belief that he/she had no alternative but to use deadly or substantial force to protect himself/herself from immanent death or great bodily harm, or to prevent a forcible felony.

Indictment: An accusatory document presented by a grand jury to the court, charging a named individual with a crime.

Intimidation: To threaten another in order to influence his behavior. The threat may include physical harm, restraint, confinement, or accusations of crime (even if true).

Jurisdiction: The geographic range of authority.

Juvenile: A person under 18 years of age.

Lockup: A temporary detention facility. While in lockup, the prisoner is photographed and fingerprinted.

M.O.: Abbreviation for modus operandi, Latin for method of operation. The pattern of behavior which is typical of how a particular offender commits a specific type of crime. Example: An offender who always wears dark glasses when robbing banks.

Manslaughter: Unlawfully killing a human being without malice.

Manslaughter, Voluntary: Killing a human being with the intent to kill or do serious bodily injury, or with a conscious disregard of an extreme risk of death or serious bodily injury, where the presence of mitigating factors (e.g. acting in the heat of passion caused by adequate provocation) precludes a determination that the killing was malicious.

Manslaughter, Involuntary: An unintentional or accidental killing without justification or excuse.

Minor: In the criminal context, a person under the age of 18 years. Also see juvenile.

Misdemeanor: An offense punishable by one year of imprisonment or less.

Murder, First Degree: The killing of another with the specific intent to kill that person, with premeditation and deliberation, and without self-defense or mitigation.

Murder, Second Degree: The killing of another with the specific intent to kill or seriously injure that person, or acted in conscious disregard of an extreme risk of death or serious bodily injury to that person, and without self-defense or mitigation.

Negligent Homicide: The killing of another as a result of the careless, reckless, or negligent operation of a motor vehicle.

Offense: A violation of the criminal law of a state or local jurisdiction.

Petty Offense: An offense for which the only allowable penalty is a fine.

Polygraph: A lie detector.

Possession of a Controlled Substance: Knowingly and intentionally possessing a controlled substance.

Probable Cause: Where known facts and circumstances, of a reasonably trustworthy nature, are sufficient to justify a man of reasonable caution or prudence in the belief that a certain person has committed, is committing, or is about to commit a criminal act.

Problem: A problem suitable for police/community resolution has the following characteristics: it is a group of related incidents; it affects a number of people; it is unlikely to disappear without intervention; a number of people agree to work on it; and it can be impacted with available resources.

Prosecutor: An attorney who brings a criminal action against a person in the name of the government.

Radar: Portable unit used by officers to determine speeds of approaching vehicles in the field.

Rape: The crime of sexual intercourse with a subject by force or threat of force, against the will and without the consent of the subject.

Reasonable Suspicion: A combination of specific facts and circumstances that would justify a reasonable officer to believe that a certain person had committed, is committing, or is about to commit a criminal; more than a hunch or mere speculation but less than probable cause necessary to arrest.

Recidivist: A repeat offender.

Roll Call: The first part of a watch or tour, reserved for attendance, inspection, briefings, and training.

Search Warrant: A written order signed by a judge authorizing an officer to search for and seize property that constitutes evidence of commission of a crime.

Sexual Abuse: Engaging in a sexual act or sexual contact with another person with knowledge or reason to know that the act was committed without that other person's permission

Shoplifting: (1) Knowingly concealing or taking possession of personal property of another that offered for sale; or (2) removing or altering the price tag, serial number or other identification mark imprinted on or attached to personal property of another, which was offered for sale; or (3) transferring any personal property of another, which was offered for sale, from the container in which it was displayed or packaged to any other display container or sales package.

Statute of Limitations: The period of time within which lawsuits or criminal prosecutions must be brought, after which it is barred for lapse of time. There is no limitation on when a prosecution can be brought for murder.

Theft: Wrongfully obtaining or using the property of another person with the intent of depriving the person of a right to the property or appropriate the property to his or her own use or to the use of another person.

Traffic Ticket: Ticket issued by a police office for a traffic infraction that one can either pay or appear in court to plead or argue.

Trajectory: The path a bullet or other flying object takes.

Unlawful Entry: Intentionally entering or attempting to enter a building without lawful authority and against the will of the occupant or the person in charge of the premises.

Verbatim: Word for word.

VIN: Abbreviation for "vehicle identification number," a unique identifier assigned when the vehicle is manufactured.

 Warrant: A written order issued by a judge that directs a law enforcement officer to arrest a person and bring them to court.

Witness: One who testifies as to what they have seen, heard, or otherwise observed and who is not necessarily a party to the action.

Youth: A person under the age of 18, also referred to as a juvenile.

About the MTA Bridges and Tunnels

MTA Bridges and Tunnels is officially known as the Triborough Bridge and Tunnel Authority, is an agency of the Metropolitan Transportation Authority, that operates seven bridges and two tunnels in New York City. The MTA Bridges & Tunnels serve more than a million people each day and take in a billion dollars in toll revenue annually.

MTA Bridge & Tunnels
Robert F. Kennedy Bridge (formerly Triborough Bridge), connecting Manhattan, the Bronx, Queens, and Randall's and Wards Islands.
Bronx–Whitestone Bridge, connecting the Bronx and Queens.
Verrazano–Narrows Bridge, connecting Brooklyn and Staten Island.
Throgs Neck Bridge, connecting Queens and the Bronx
Henry Hudson Bridge, connecting Manhattan and the Bronx
Gil Hodges Memorial Bridge (formerly Marine Park Bridge), connecting Brooklyn and Queens
Cross Bay Bridge, connecting the Rockaways to mainland Queens.
Hugh L. Carey Tunnel (formerly Brooklyn–Battery Tunnel), connecting Brooklyn and Manhattan
Queens–Midtown Tunnel, connecting Queens and Manhattan

The Triborough Bridge and Tunnel Authority has 1000 Bridge and Tunnel Officers, who are NYS Peace Officers authorized to make arrests and carry firearms on and off duty. B & T Officers patrol the authority's facilities. Besides law enforcement, the officers collect tolls, assist vehicles stuck in E-ZPass lanes, operate tow trucks to clear disabled vehicles, and clear snow from the roadways.

WITHDRAWN

14.02   12/5/16.

LONGWOOD PUBLIC LIBRARY
800 Middle Country Road
Middle Island, NY 11953
(631) 924-6400
longwoodlibrary.org

LIBRARY HOURS

Monday-Friday	9:30 a.m. - 9:00 p.m.
Saturday	9:30 a.m. - 5:00 p.m.
Sunday (Sept-June)	1:00 p.m. - 5:00 p.m.

57713249R00120

Made in the USA
Lexington, KY
27 November 2016